Measuring the ROI of Knowledge Management

2nd edition

EDITED BY EDWARD BOWES

Head of events and books
Leah Darbyshire

Commissioning editor
Laura Slater

Editorial assistant
Edward Bowes

Published by
Globe Law and Business Ltd
3 Mylor Close
Horsell
Woking
Surrey GU21 4DD
United Kingdom
Tel: +44 20 3745 4770
www.globelawandbusiness.com

ISBN: 978-1-78358-268-6
A catalogue record for this book is available from the British Library

Contents

Executive summary

For organisations looking at knowledge management (KM), it is no longer a question of 'should we?' It is now a question of '*how* should we?' KM has been accepted as an integral practice for most organisations – however many are still, understandably, cautious of the investments they make in the current financial environment following the economic downturn.

The intangible nature of knowledge resources has proven to be a difficult issue for organisations to tackle. It is no easy process to ascertain the value of an unquantifiable resource, which makes it difficult to justify investment in KM. As David Griffiths remarks in chapter one: 'The measurement of knowledge value is difficult. It is specific to time, context, and the perception of what it is that constitutes a knowledge asset.' So, what is the best course of action for an organisation looking to prove the value of their KM efforts?

Measuring the ROI of Knowledge Management 2nd edition aims to explore how leading industry experts prove the value of their KM initiatives and justify investing in them. From outlining the best methods of quantifying the return from KM, to discussing the limitations of an ROI-focused approach, this book looks to present an all-encompassing view of how to best tackle this this matter that is rife with guesswork and uncertainty.

David Griffiths, founder of K3-Cubed, starts the book off with an introduction to the 'knowledge economy'; outlining what the key economic drivers of KM are, how KM can create a competitive advantage, and why it is so difficult to measure it's value.

Moving into part one, the book focuses on the quantifying of knowledge assets, and the returns they bring. In chapter two James Gunn, charted engineer and knowledge management consultant, explores the varying business case arguments that can be made to justify a KM programme, and identifies their strengths and weaknesses. Examples of these include; the creation of new markets, capitalising on a strategic advantage, and maintaining legal obligations. In chapter three, Tim Hawley, associate director of Arup, explains the process of designing and utilising a 'knowledge audit' to not only determine exactly what knowledge exists in an organisation, but also determine how best to drive a positive ROI from the defined assets.

The next biggest step in technological improvement for many organisations is the successful integration of artificial intelligence (AI) into their business practices. Chapter four moves to address the incoming issue of AI as a knowledge asset, with James Loft, chief executive officer at Matter AI, discussing how AI can affect the KM space by adding value, and how it can ultimately support in delivering a good return on KM investments.

Chapter five features Hélène Russell, founder of TheKnowledge Business, giving an overview of the best practical methods for measuring KM projects to better understand their positive impacts and their 'value for money'; showing how to use the 'balanced scorecard' to ensure a balanced view of all measurement systems, and the 10 key 'design tests' that a measurement system should aim to fulfil.

Part two of the book then moves into outlining the limitations of a solely ROI-focused approach to understanding the value of KM projects, giving light to other approaches that allow room for the intangible nature of knowledge resources. Chapter six features John Hovell, head of organisational development at BAE systems, explaining how looking at the ROI is only useful to a certain point, and is more effective when used in conjunction with other measurement efforts; such as the use of anecdotal evidence of organisational wins.

In chapter seven, Stan Garfield, knowledge management author, speaker, and community leader, proposes arguments against the measurement of the ROI of KM – outlining that focusing on the benefits and progress of KM project is a more helpful approach. This leads into a literature review of more leading industry experts outlining the issues and limitations of ROI-based measurements.

In chapter eight Andrew Gent, lead information architect at VoltDB, gives an overview of how supporting and nurturing the on-going investment in KM is a more effective and healthy method of approaching and tackling value, as justifying the ROI in a one-off case often works against the project that is trying to be implemented. Tips for keeping the project safe from being axed by budget reviews are outlined; including embedding KM into an organisation's daily operations and designing the KM initiative to cost as little as possible by repurposing existing resources.

Finally, in chapter nine, Professor Dave Snowden, chief scientific officer of Cognitive Edge, offers an explanation of the differences between outcome, output, and vector measurements – and how holding explicit goals that are tracked can destroy the intrinsic motivation behind the project. He then moves to outline newer approaches that are emerging to deal with systems and resources that are both intangible and uncertain.

About the authors

Stan Garfield is a knowledge manager, communities of practice evangelist, community facilitator, collaboration and social media specialist, social business practitioner, author, speaker, and leader based in Northville, Michigan. He has worked in the field of knowledge management for over 20 years.

Stan spent eight years at Deloitte leading communities and enterprise social networking. Prior to that, he spent 25 years at HP, Compaq, and Digital Equipment Corporation.

Stan launched Digital's first knowledge management programme in 1996, helped develop the corporate KM strategy for Compaq, and led the Worldwide Consulting & Integration Knowledge Management Program for HP. He also worked for PricewaterhouseCoopers, St. Louis University School of Medicine, and Washington University School of Medicine.

Stan holds a BS in Applied Mathematics and Computer Science from Washington University in St. Louis. He leads the SIKM Leaders Community with over 600 members globally, and is invited to present at numerous conferences, including KMWorld. Stan has published over 100 LinkedIn articles on leadership, innovation, knowledge management, communities of practice, enterprise social networks, and social media.

Andrew Gent has 30 years experience working in knowledge management and information architecture for everything from large global corporations to first round startups. His focus is the intersection of knowledge and usability. He is currently the lead information architect at VoltDB Inc. He is also the author of a book of poetry, *[explicit lyrics]*, which won the 2016 Miller Williams Prize.

David Griffiths, PhD (Edin), MSc (Edin), CMgr FCMI is a popular international speaker, consultant, and founder of K3-Cubed Limited. K3 is a University of Edinburgh start-up company (now independent, but funded by the University in 2009 as a result of proprietary knowledge management research conducted by David), focused on consulting and development solutions for organisations facing challenges in the areas of strategy, knowledge management, learning and development, HR agility, complexity, and resilience.

K3-Cubed has delivered services for organisations as diverse as Maybank (Malaysia), the Bahrain Government, Scottish Water, the Scottish Government, Fife Police, Ubisoft, Bahrain Natural Gas, Indiana CPA Society, Georgia CPA Society, Mars Inc., Quintiles Pharmaceuticals (Europe and APAC operations), Middle East NGOs, US top 400 accounting firms, the University of Glamorgan, British Aerospace, University of Wales Trinity Saint David, Visa (Europe), the Water Research Centre (UK), EcoPetrol (Colombia), Juran Benchmarking, Atomic Weapons Establishment (UK), European Institute of Innovation and Technology, Abbot Vascular, the Water Research Centre, TallyFox Social Technologies (Switzerland), CPA Society Executives Association (USA), DuPont, Kaleo Technologies (USA), the European Training Foundation, and the English Institute of Sport.

David holds a PhD in knowledge management and an MSc in the Management of Training and Development, both from the University of Edinburgh. David is also a chartered fellow with the Chartered Management Institute.

David's work won an Emerald Literati Network Award for Research Excellence in 2012. In December 2011 he was recognised as one of four key worldwide influencers in the knowledge management field. In 2013 he was listed him as one of the top 30 knowledge management influencers in the world ('Top 100 names to know in KM'). In 2014 his knowledge management and organisational learning project with the Indiana Certified Public Accountants Society (INCPAS) won a 'best project' award at the Society of Association Executives annual awards. In 2014 he wrote a book on HR development for the United States accounting profession, which was recommended by the American Institute of Certified Public Accountants as a top read for the profession. In 2015 he was again named as one of the top 10 influencers in the field of knowledge management. In 2016 David won the Chartered Management Institute Management Article of the Year Award for his article on leadership, decision-making, and change management – and the prestigious ASAE Power of 'A' Elite Summit Award for the CPA CoE project (Indiana).

James Gunn is a chartered engineer and has been a knowledge management consultant for 15 years. He has led knowledge management programmes in large organisations including government ministries and the aerospace, electronics, telecoms, and not-for-profit sectors. He has a broad understanding of business, knowledge management, and knowledge technology gained from experience as well as from working as an associate lecturer for the Open University Business School. He now leads KM programme implementations for Tacit Connexions, a knowledge systems integrator. James regularly speaks and writes on knowledge management and knowledge technology. James is a member of the BSI's working group on ISO 30401 (the Knowledge Management Standard)

Tim Hawley is an experienced consultant and facilitator, advising on knowledge management, organisational change, and business performance improvement – focusing on improving organisational effectiveness and delivering value from complex integrated change programmes.

Tim works with organisations to help shape their thinking around how best to leverage their intellectual capital and align their knowledge management programmes with their business objectives, enabling organisations to better adapt to their rapidly changing environments by adopting new ways of working and building organisational resilience.

Tim has over 30 years of experience across the private, public, and third sector, and has led a series of major knowledge management and organisational transformation programmes, often internationally and particularly across Asia.

Tim is an associate director of Arup, an independent firm owned in trust on behalf of its staff of designers, planners, engineers, consultants, and technical specialists; and globally recognised for its award-winning approach to knowledge management.

John Hovell is BAE Systems' head of organisational development (OD), and a practitioner, speaker, and author in OD and KM strategy and methods. John led a team to win a Chairman's Award at BAE Systems in 2014. Previously, John was part of a team to win the prestigious NOVA award, Lockheed Martin's top recognition award, for accomplishments related to knowledge management. Additionally, he was instrumental in the creation and execution of the enterprise KM strategy for ManTech International Corporation.

John volunteered as the corporate lead for the award-winning annual STEMmerday event where thousands of participants engaged in science, technology, engineering, and math-related learning activities. John serves on several advisory boards including the International Knowledge Management Institute, Training Industry Quarterly, and Synergy Development and Training.

John has led or been a member of five different teams that have won awards from *Chief Learning Officer magazine*. In 2015, he was named the eighth most influential person in knowledge management. He published a chapter in a book titled *Making It Real: Sustaining Knowledge Management*. In 2009, he was honoured by *Training Magazine* as one of the 'Top Young Trainers'. In 2007, he earned his Certified Knowledge Manager (CKM) certification from the International Knowledge Management Institute. He earned his Project Management Professional (PMP) from the Project Management Institute (PMI) in 2005. He earned his master's degree from The George Washington University in Washington, D.C. and his undergraduate degree from Virginia Tech in Blacksburg, Virginia, USA.

James Loft is a graduate of knowledge management from Loughborough University and has worked extensively in innovation and new technologies in transport and financial services, culminating in the running of an artificial intelligence consultancy firm that helps companies make AI tools fit their businesses rather than the other way around. His mission is to de-mystify the world of 'Applied AI' for organisations and users to level the playing field for the progression of the technology now, rather than as a vision for the future.

With an experienced background in innovation and service design he understands the gentle but vital balance between the design and the technology, and advocates an MVP style approach to new technology in order to achieve success.

An active member of a community of AI companies, tools, and platforms, James possesses a broad understanding of the possibilities the technologies can offer and will support in their implementation where possible to advance the marketplace.

Hélène Russell of TheKnowledgeBusiness specialises in helping organisations to grow and improve profitability, by helping them to understand and improve their knowledge systems. Hélène is the author of the Law Society's *Knowledge Management Handbook* and Legal Monitor's *Practical Projects in Legal KM*. She teaches open and in-house courses in knowledge management and also offers coaching, mentoring, and advice. She also runs Knowledge Network UK, the only regional knowledge sharing and networking group for law firm KMers in UK.

Hélène has spoken extensively on KM for Ark, Butterworths, UWE, Bristol Law Society, Allice, and at Knowledge Network UK, and has written regularly for *Managing Partner Magazine*. After a decade as a solicitor with a major regional firm specialising in clinical negligence defence litigation, eight years in knowledge management and having recently obtained an MBA with distinction, she has a unique, deep understanding of how knowledge flows helps law firms and professional services organisations.

Professor Snowden is director of the Cynefin Centre at Bangor University and chief scientific officer of Cognitive Edge. Formerly a director of the IBM Institute for knowledge management he pioneered an organic approach to the field and was identified by Thomas Stewart, former editor of the HBR as one of the leading thinkers on tacit knowledge. He received a special award from the Academy of Management for his contribution to the field and his paper 'Complex Acts of Knowing' is one of the ten most cited articles in the subject.

Chapter 1: **Understanding the knowledge economy**

By David Griffiths, founder of K3-Cubed

This report will often refer to the knowledge economy, which is a general term with multiple definitions aimed at describing modern economic challenges. It is an economy driven by the use, diffusion, and creation of knowledge.

This leads towards the application of knowledge as an economic resource. The deputy secretary general of the OECD[1] stated that competitive advantage is grounded in the ability of an organisation to be more efficient and effective than its competitors, with knowledge being something that needs to be harnessed to exploit the uniqueness of the organisation. It is this uniqueness that is of interest to organisations seeking competitive advantage, but it is the management of knowledge resources that is the biggest challenge facing organisations today. Organisations are operating in a global economy, characterised by the emergence of intellectual capital as a core value driver as the following statistics infer:

- The value of intangible resources has dramatically increased over the past 80 years, rising from a 30 per cent representation of company valuation in 1929 to recent times where companies such as Google and Microsoft have declared intangible assets to be worth as much as 90 per cent;[2]
- Intellectual capital has been found to account for 78 per cent of the value on the Standard & Poor's 500;[3] and
- In a 2010 analysis of the US stock market performance of 79 companies across service, manufacturing, and financial sectors between 1998-2003, it was found that the mere announcement of a strategy to manage knowledge resources could have a significant positive impact on an organisation's market value.[4]

The message is clear: knowledge is valuable, but the strategic value drivers embedded in the knowledge economy are hard to define. This has to be understood if an organisation is to justify investment in KM projects. What is the point in investing in KM processes unless they address strategic and operational needs? How can an organisation address KM unless it understands the drivers that impact the concept?

Economic value drivers

Without doubt, strategic value exists in developing a unique position for the organisation as it transacts in the knowledge economy – an economy that the OECD[5] describes as having four pillars (refer to Figure 1):

- Innovation (or knowledge-creation) – As a critical factor of competitive advantage;
- New technologies – Linking technology progress to growth in productivity;
- Human capital – Seen as essential to harness the benefits of the first two pillars; and
- Enterprise dynamics – Also known as adaptive capacity, the ability to flex according to evolving consumer needs.

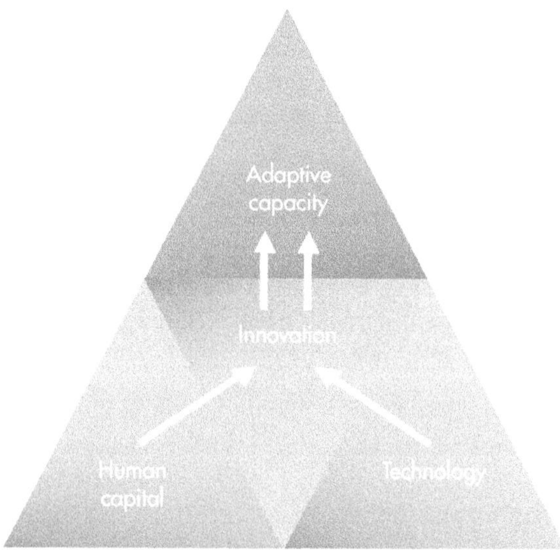

Fundamentally, the basis of the knowledge economy is human capital: the socialisation of human resources being a key to innovation and the development of organisational adaptive capacity. When was the last time technology spontaneously created knowledge? Take away people and gauge how effective technology is at creating dynamic capability in the organisation.

In the view of this report, while technology is a founding aspect of the pyramid, it cannot be enabled without the intervention of people, which is why human capital (people) is seen as the pivotal aspect of the knowledge economy and an organisation's competitive advantage. To enable this and produce value-driven adaptive capacity, a constant state of development is required – the only constant for a knowledge-centric organisation is change, as Thomas Clarke infers in *The Knowledge Economy:* 'In dynamic environments highly developed learning is necessary in order to keep knowledge current; an organisation's learning capability must keep pace with the changes in the competitive environment.'[6]

This idea of an organisation's 'learning capability informing adaptive capacity' links knowledge to the learning capacity of an organisation, a concept that will be discussed later in this report.

Develop a competitive advantage

The theoretical arguments surrounding the views in the proceeding paragraphs are contentious. It is not the intention of this report to bring resolution to these arguments, only to report on the concepts and use their currency to develop potential benefits for organisational KM process.

The management of resources requires a strategy to underpin the value associated with them. Two approaches dominate the KM field: the resource based view (RBV) and the more recent knowledge based view (KBV). The two are often interchangeable during discussions on the management of knowledge for competitive advantage, but the reality is that they are different. The strategy the organisation chooses is critical as the RBV leans more towards a view of knowledge as an object, while the KBV leans more towards the view of knowledge as a process.

> *I feel strongly that you can't 'manage' knowledge, you can only manage people, environment and information. Management needs to come to a pretty serious understanding that it only has three things going for it at any organisation; people, money and information.*
>
> (KM, Australian Government)

The RBV sees costly-to-copy resources as a fundamental source of competitive advantage. Competitive advantage is founded upon the unique knowledge and skills held by the organisation, which are informed by its human capital. The RBV encourages the concept of knowledge as a transferable commodity; one where codification is encouraged under the guise of intellectual capital. In this way knowledge can be measured and controlled. The problem with this approach is that it treats physical and knowledge assets in the same way. How can the knowledge in ones head be treated as a commodity in the same way as the organisation treats a physical commodity? Perhaps this is one of the reasons Nonaka attempted to convince practitioners of the potential to transform tacit knowledge into explicit forms.

Ask yourself this: is costly-to-copy competitive advantage lost when an organisation seeks to make the knowledge that informs it explicit? These deficiencies led to the development of another concept, the KBV, within which knowledge is seen as the primary value creation tool for organisations. The KBV gives currency to the intangible value to be found in communities of practice and learning organisations, believing that people and their ability to innovate and generate dynamic capability or adaptive capacity are what create the competitive advantage for an organisation.

[There are] significant differences in perception of Asia versus westerners. [We ask], reasonably, whether the job of KM practitioners is to get Americans – or westerners – to act more Japanese. I think this is indeed what we are being asked. We are being asked, to some extent, to abandon the rugged individualism that America so prizes, in the name of group cohesion and knowledge sharing. The truth is, humans are connected creatures. Knowledge is a product of connection, in that it is, in the last analysis, socially constructed. So there is no knowledge without connection. This seems to be the essence of Nonaka's message, although he complicated the story with his model.

(Federal KM Working Group, US)

It would also seem fair to say that the RBV gives currency to the explicit view of knowledge while the KBV gives the authority to a HR-centric view of knowledge. There is also strong debate as to the theoretical validity of the KBV of the firm. In practical terms (the most important thing to KM leaders) however, it appears to have operational validity while also speaking to the drivers of the knowledge economy. For that reason it is given currency by this report and is seen as a viable way to conceptualise the blended need of technology (explicit) and human resource (tacit) driven knowledge strategies.

Measuring the value of knowledge

Don't get excited – there is no miraculous solution offered here, only reality. The measurement of knowledge value is difficult. It is specific to time, context, and the perception of what it is that constitutes a knowledge asset. This will vary according to organisation and sector. For some, they are tangible (objects) such as patents, discrete, or intangible – being deposited in people, processes, culture, and structure. These discrete assets make the development of metrics for the measurement of knowledge value difficult and subjective.

> *How can you measure what's in my head? I know what I know and the only way I can measure it is by winning contracts. Then, I suppose, I can put a value on what I know. But, if a client asked me to value what one of their employee's knows, I wouldn't know where to begin!*
>
> (Company director, UK)

Human intellect and character are difficult to measure both individually and socially, which will hinder organisations when attempting to place a value on the knowledge held by their people. Not only this, but the valuation of the existence of a knowledge asset is one thing, but what about the costs of managing that asset? How does the impact of that process affect the valuation of the asset? This makes the task of determining return on investment from KM activity a daunting one.

> *In this age the true assets of companies are the knowledge stores in their employee's minds. They must use it strategically to compete with their rivals.*
>
> (KM practitioner, India)

Attempts to predict the value of KM initiatives are often based on guesswork, where historical precedents are projected forward to predict future value. However, how can an organisation predict the impact of outliers that will, perhaps, change strategy and become a new source of competitive advantage and value? For example, when the internet was initially conceived and developed, who could have predicted the value associated with its commercial application or its omnipotent place in modern society? When it comes to KM, practitioners are left to either rely on methods such as critical incident technique, to measure the consequences of past action or non-action and forecast them into the future, or they speak in terms of gut instinct.

We just know what we need and trust
that it will be of benefit.
(UK operations of a US-based MNE)

The value-based decision-making process that informs the need to engage with KM can be explained at a macro level within the organisation, using the drivers of the knowledge economy within which the organisation transacts. And while the development of return on investment metrics is complex, contextual, time-related, and impossible to capture in this report, the following paragraphs are offered as a foundation for macro KM value discussions in organisations.

First there are the drivers of the knowledge economy, which require an organisation to become dynamic and in doing so acknowledge the synergy between people, knowledge, and learning. This inevitably leads to conversations on the relationship between organisational value and social capital – the value brought about by social processes and culture that bind the organisation's human resources as they interact with internal and external stakeholders. Figure 2 takes a generic intellectual capital model[7] and aligns it with the OECD's pillars of the knowledge economy. This is designed to show KM leaders how capital structures come together to develop overall market value. The objective of this type of illustration is to bolster clarity of thought when discussing how intangible KM processes can contribute to the market value of an organisation. A good example of what is being discussed in the development of social capital is Pfizerpedia, Pfizer pharmaceutical's knowledge platform.

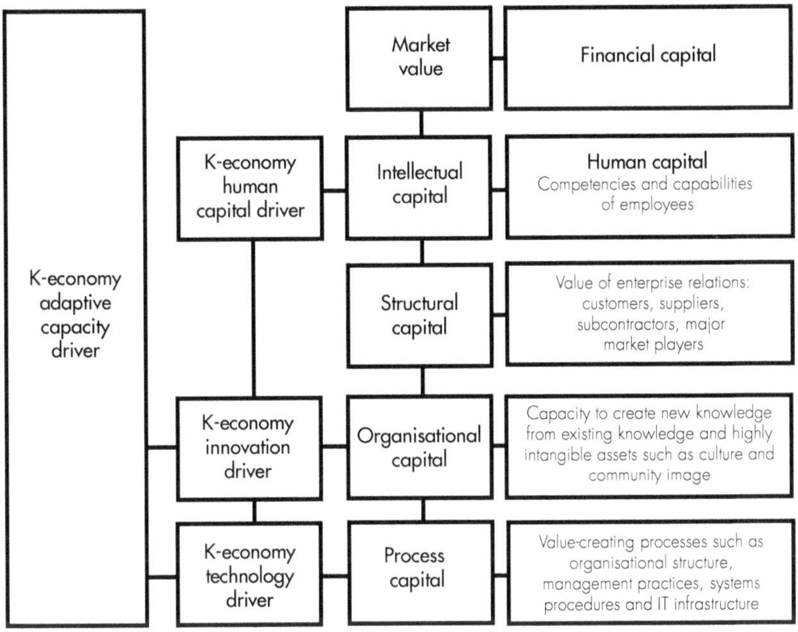

Pfizerpedia is an integrated wiki, social networking, and storage network that enables the sharing of know-who and know-what within the Pfizer organisation. It enables the networking of employees to maximise the impact of communities of practice and heightens the visibility of individual knowledge artefacts through blogging, Wiki, and tagging tools. It is not within the scope of this report to bring a critical examination of this platform; the only intention is to introduce readers to an example of the application of technology within the workplace. At the time of writing this report an overview of the Pfizerpedia called 'Meet Jessica' was publicly available on the internet through the following link: http://www.slideshare.net/bengardner135/meet-jessica

Summary

This section has attempted to provide an insight into the value of knowledge as a resource. It has identified links between knowledge and the market value of an organisation. It has also established the value of knowledge as a resource within the RBV or KBV of the organisation, driven by the needs of the knowledge economy. It has attempted to demonstrate the complexity of the issues surrounding the KM concept and to emphasise that people are a pivotal resource in the development of an organisation's dynamic capability or adaptive capacity. This leads to the issue of the management of these resources.

Currently, KM is facing a multitude of problems and issues, many of which are discussed extensively in this report. There has been a gradual shift in terminology in relation to KM, brought about to meet the shifting needs of the environment, but the core need to utilise knowledge endures. It therefore stands to reason that KM itself will have to undergo a shift, especially if the field fails to overcome the dominance of technology-based KM solutions. But, regardless of what it might be called in the future, however it reinvents itself, historical precedent indicates that organisations will continue to need to manage knowledge as a resource for value creation. The key message in this chapter is to forget about the KM label and focus on the need of the organisation and the environment within which the organisation transacts. That need dictates what action is required and the label placed on that action really does not matter; as long as the action and the outcome meet the organisation's need. Given the drivers of the knowledge economy and the need for adaptive capacity, it is fair to say that the only constant for sustainable success is change.

A version of this article first appeared in Griffiths, D. Redefining KM: New Principles for Better Practice, *London: ARK Group, 2011.*

References

1. Ásgeirsdottir, B., 'OECD/NSF conference on 'Advancing knowledge and the knowledge economy', OECD work on knowledge and the knowledge economy', National Academies, Washington DC, 10-11 January 2005.
2. Ash, J., 'Why isn't knowledge working?', Scientific computing, May 2001; retrieved on 17 August 2007.
3. Call, D., 'Knowledge Management – not rocket science', Journal of Knowledge Management, 9(2) pp19-30, 2005.
4. Choi, B., & Jong, A.M., 'Assessing the impact of knowledge management strategies announcements on the market value of firms', Information and management, 47(1) pp42–52, 2010.
5. Ásgeirsdottir, ibid.
6. Clarke, T., 'The knowledge economy', Education and training journal, Volume 43(4/5), pp189-196, 2001.
7. Diakoulakis, I.E., Georpopoulos, N.B., Koulouriotis, D.E., & Emeris, D.M., 'Towards a holistic knowledge management model', Journal of Knowledge Management, 8(1), pp32–46, 2004.

Chapter 2:
Knowledge management business case arguments

By James Gunn, chartered engineer and knowledge management consultant

There are as many kinds of business cases and ROI calculations as there are knowledge management projects, and each one is unique. In a previous paper published by ARK, I talked about the specific problems of justifying knowledge management programmes, which I identified as:

- **Executive scepticism** – KM programmes have a poor record of successful delivery;
- **"Wicked" problem potential** – the tendency of KM programmes to degenerate into a source of conflict, confusion, and become a moving target;
- **KM, a multi-disciplinary discipline** – there is no shared understanding of knowledge or knowledge management; and
- **Linking KM with the resulting benefits** – this takes effort and many don't accept the analysis.

The arguments that you can make in justifying your KM programme will depend on the nature of your programme. As there are so many knowledge management approaches, I'll try to categorise them to some extent, show the kind of arguments that you can make in their support, and then look at the strengths and weaknesses of the arguments.

KM – It's the law/in the contract

Of course, these business cases are easy but not that common. They mostly apply to heavily regulated industries and impose a legal duty on an asset owner or design authority to ensure that the necessary knowledge for the safe operation and maintenance of the asset is maintained. Examples include operators of nuclear power stations and the manufacturers of civil aircraft.

You may remember the crash of Concorde in Paris in 2000. It took two years to redesign and implement straightforward changes; much of this time was spent finding the long retired design engineers to re-establish the original design rationale (a regulatory requirement) before making design changes. At £8,000 per return ticket, 100 passengers for each daily flight and seven Concordes, BA lost quite a lot of revenue.

As nuclear plants age, knowledge retention is becoming an increasing problem for nuclear plant operators – re-designing systems means huge costs of re-justifying safety cases and that means expensive simulation modelling.

Obviously even the finance director is not sceptical of the operating licence conditions or legal contracts, but he or she will push back if the scope of the business case goes beyond "the necessary knowledge". A separate case may be needed for further KM work which would not be legally or contractually required, but if successful with a "necessary knowledge" first phase, then successful initial phase work will make justifying further phases easier.

Creating new markets

One of the most stunning changes in recent times has been the introduction of the smartphone. Apple went from niche desktop computer provider to world's biggest company (by stock market valuation) in a few years by launching the smartphone. While the smartphone didn't need any new technology to be developed, it did create new markets for mobile apps and mobile advertising. I would argue that Apple created this product from their knowledge of markets, of a variety of electronic components, and of software to realise a vision of a phone as phone-cum-computer. Not all new markets are created so quickly. Other brands associated with new markets include Uber, Sony's Walkman, Intuit's financial software, Lexus cars, Amazon (how many do you want), Dyson, and Starbucks – they have all created new markets by creating a new combination of value from a new combination of their knowledge of customers, production processes, and technology. While start-ups may find this easier, large companies sometimes use this as a business strategy. Creating a business case is about calculating the potential value of the market, the chances of success and the cost of doing so. The biggest uncertainty will be in the chances of success.

Creating a unique capability

One of the reasons that people continue to advocate knowledge management programmes is the belief that unique knowledge creates unique capabilities for which customers are willing to pay and which cannot be duplicated quickly by competitors.

A few years ago, Airbus developed a new way of configuring their aircraft to each airline's requirements. By capturing the process knowledge for wing rib manufacture and implementing it in software, Airbus could redesign wing ribs in hours instead of months. It thus became feasible to offer customers a more fuel efficient batch of aircraft. Since this reduced fuel consumption by several per cent, Airbus has gained significant market share from competition over the last fifteen years.

If creating this unique capability has been a burning desire of the organisation, then justifying it will be about cash flow, time, and feasibility; and not ROI. Think of Nuclear Fusion, long recognised as the next good way of generating electricity, but while nobody doubts that one day we will use it, we're always told that we're still about 30 years away, and that seems to deter any serious investment in making it work.

However, building a consensus about the need for such a capability and its feasibility may take a long time. Unique Capabilities are often created in Process rather than Product or Service. Unique Capabilities will usually create significant increases in market share; by talking to a sample of the customers, you can assess how large that change might be and what the increased revenue (and costs naturally) will be – there's your investment case.

Creating strategic advantage

Somewhere between Creating a Unique Capability and Incremental Improvement is the Strategic Advantage. This may be achieved by breakthroughs in performance (20–30 per cent) either in Process or Product/Service. A knowledge driven strategic advantage may be easier to copy than a Unique Capability, but in the meantime it is reasonable to assume that gains in market share, revenue, pricing power, and cost savings are available – while the business case's ROI is likely to be overwhelmingly in favour of the KM project.

Improving process productivity/incremental improvement

Many kinds of KM project operate in this zone, including:

- **Process led** KM initiatives (how do they differ from process improvement projects?)
- **Training led** programmes (knowledge workers with the right skills will be more productive)

- **Information Science** (if you store information right, the next person can re-use that information and that'll be faster than reinventing the wheel)
- **Information Technology** (if you have the right tools, usually search engines, you can find knowledge more quickly and thus be more productive)

The gain in productivity must obviously be greater than the cost of process change/training/information management/information technology. Typically, high single figure percentage improvements in productivity are achieved. Arguments can be made along these lines:

- Once Process Owners have accepted your assumptions about available improvements, arguing a process productivity case is just arithmetic.
- Cost of Quality arguments may be useful here – they depend on increasing Right First Time rate and eliminating lots of rework.
- Improved Customer Satisfaction may result in higher values of Customer Lifetime Value (segment by segment), increased referrals and incremental market share gains.
- Where knowledge can be implemented in system, the productivity often arises from the use of less senior/experienced staff with their lower charge out rates and lower overhead costs.

Measuring process productivity before and after change is a long and controversial business as all bench markers know.

The business must convince your KM Programme Board that the changes you will introduce will lead to the process improvements. There may be a number of other objections:

- The cost of these projects means that the productivity gain will need to be significant to achieve a return on the investment. Gains are exponentially difficult to realise (i.e. two times gains means more than twice the effort/expense)
- Running a pilot training programme doesn't work – those who have been trained revert to old behaviour when surrounded by untrained colleagues. On the other hand, running a large programme disrupts normal business and everybody knows next quarters figures are the most important thing.

- Information Science/Management (what librarians do) is very useful when people share an understanding of the classification system in use, or when professionals are on hand to sort problems out. Anyone who has looked at the personal storage areas of an organisation knows that everyone sorts information in a very personal way – taxonomies not only don't work, but they scare most people out of their wits. You probably won't be asked something like 'Why are we trying to use Information Science to manage knowledge?'.
- Information Technology – many clever ways to search information and data have been developed. Semantic technology is becoming better, but all these IT approaches are still treating KM as an information problem. Most KM Boards will need a lot of convincing that;
    - IT can solve a knowledge problem (Arguably using IT for KM has earned KM its reputation); and
    - A successful pilot will become easier and more beneficial as you roll it out more widely and deeply.

Lessons learned programmes

Lessons Learned programmes are common in organisations with project operations. Between project phases and at project end, there is usually a short time window allowing reflection on the project's progress. Continuous process operation tends to be fine-tuned already.

Lessons Learned programmes have a better track record of success than other KM approaches and have the advantage of an acknowledged problem and in most cases a well understood way of addressing them. Especially in the initial stages, Lessons Learned initiatives tend to concentrate on putting right bigger failures, but as lessons are learned it is inevitable that the fruit has to be picked from higher up the tree.

In the early stages, the big lessons can be appraised individually and treated as stand-alone projects. As the programme advances, the lessons will get smaller, which means that the basis of the investment appraisal will shift away from project appraisals towards Cost Of (Poor) Quality arguments as the lessons address more frequent, smaller failures.

Cost of Quality costs are assessed in four groups:

- Internal failure costs – costs which arise if the defect is detected before the customer receives the product/service (e.g. waste, scrap, rework, and failure analysis).

- External failure costs – costs associated with defects detected after the customer receives the product/service (e.g. repairs/servicing, warranty claims, complaints, and returns).
- Appraisal costs – the cost of determining conformance (or not) (e.g. verification of requirements, quality audits, supplier assessment).
- Prevention costs – the cost of avoiding failure and appraisal (e.g. specification preparation, quality planning and assurance, training).

Cost of Quality means looking at each stage of a process, measuring the rates of particular failures, estimating their values, and then multiplying by the number of times the process is initiated. This figure is a maximum – it will not be possible to eliminate all defects, and some of the changes introduced to avoid defects will have a cost too. A Cost of Quality (CoQ) based business case would have to justify the inclusion of some CoQs and the exclusion of others.

For the purposes of appraising an investment in a knowledge management programme, the CoQ value must be replaced by the "Cost of Ignorance". I coin this term in the sense of the dictionary definition (not common usage) as shorthand for 'valuing those defects arising from lack of knowledge' and no judgements about people's character or intellectual capabilities are intended or implied. The Cost of Ignorance calculation will have similar elements (internal, external, appraisal, and prevention costs).

Encouraging knowledge sharing

Knowledge management programmes based on Social Networks, Communities of Practice, or Culture Change are more common. Generally speaking, they have low capital costs because they use existing software in a new way, open source software, or no software at all. The ongoing costs aren't attributed to KM programmes because they are now 'just part of the job'!

These programmes often rely on justifications which sound a bit like:

> *If enough of us network with enough other members of the organisation, then useful knowledge exchanges will occur more often and we hope that these extra knowledge exchanges will be worth more to the organisation than all the time we spend networking.*

It is completely obvious that knowledge management is worth doing, here are some examples (of large benefits) from other organisations.
Managing knowledge is no different from managing finance or managing people and yet Finance and HR don't have to produce an ROI.

Whether you agree with such arguments or not, if they are to succeed then the organisation's change programme governance will have to be changed or waived.

If such a programme does proceed, then claiming of benefits will depend on someone in the business being willing to give credit where credit is due, and this is less common than you'd expect. You may then have some examples of large benefits, but if KM activities are taking everybody even one hour a week, then many large benefits will be needed to offset these costs.

The accurate collection of costs or benefits from this kind of programme is always going be difficult. Many line managers will see this as giving licence to staff to work on someone else's project.

KM in support departments

KM isn't just useful to the day to day operations of Sales and Operations. It is also useful to departments that create the organisation's future such as Strategy, Procurement (not Purchasing), and Product Development.

Knowledge management in strategy

Perhaps the most influential knowledge workers live in Corporate Strategy. They diagnose corporate problems, design solutions, and then plan the implementation of those solutions.

Perhaps the Strategy Lifecycle has the following stages:

- Strategic Intent – competitive analysis, market analysis, SWOT, etc.
- Define To-Be Business Model – To-Be model of the desired end state.
- Strategic Roadmap – route from As-Is to the To-Be, includes way points and dependencies on external events and internal cohesion. Includes high level change programme/plan and governance.
- Strategic Review – how is it going/did it go?
- Rinse and Repeat.

And corporate strategy benefits are probably:

- Strategic Alignment – are we all rowing in the same direction?
- Corporate Focus and Direction – have we stopped doing the things we said we'd stop doing?
- Risk Reduction – if the worst happens, can we respond?
- Corporate Agility – if we need to, can we change?
- Corporate Positioning – are we differentiated?

A wide range of high level knowledge is needed for this task, but the fundamental how to/process knowledge will be embedded in corporate strategy processes. The feedback on the effectiveness of corporate strategy will be slow because implementation may take time and the impact of implementation will take longer. Knowledge management can:

- **Shorten the strategy lifecycle** – if we can define and implement strategy faster, we can adapt the external environment quicker;
- **Increase the capacity of the strategy process** – if more options can be generated and properly evaluated, then the strategy/change programme will be improved;
- Help to **recognise the impact** of the Strategic Change Programme – looking for and finding leading indicators of success/failure will reduce the risk of the change programme; and
- Improve the quality of **decision making** – choosing the correct strategy more often will have huge long term effects. Competitive differentiation is likely to be diluted by continual changes in strategy.

Arguments for knowledge management aren't easy to quantify, but for the small investment needed in a relatively small department, it is hardly worth saving the money. Calculate the costs and then compare it with a risk adjusted value of doing strategy badly.

Knowledge management in product development

Product Development is all about knowledge management; product portfolio managers need to have a feel for market and technology trends, the competitiveness of the current product portfolio, the organisation's own manufacturing/delivery capability, the expertise of current staff and gaps, and a robust product pipeline and know how to combine all this to churn out new products. Arguments you can make might include;

- **A better product pipeline** – If your product pipeline focuses resources on 'good' products and reduces waste by stopping development of 'bad' products then more successful products will be launched;
- **A faster product pipeline** – the rationale for being first to market is well established. It is likely to lead to greater market share and of course will reduce the cost of development. If staff need less time to develop products, then presumably the capacity of the pipeline is also increased;
- **'Better' products** – products that meet market needs will sell more, be more profitable, and will probably have a longer life. If KM can make your product pipeline better at estimating market size, at capturing and validating customer requirements, at meeting those requirements and delivering them in a manufacturable package, then your products will be 'better' and volume, profitability, and life extension arguments can all be used;
- **More products** – if you increase the capacity of your product pipeline (check downstream before claiming this benefit), then you can have a bigger portfolio and you simply use a new product business case as the return; and
- **Knowledge reuse** – development in most product pipelines is staged. When products don't make it through the later stages, it is likely that some re-usable valuable knowledge has been created. Some viable products don't make it to market for non-fundamental reasons – there may be market demand and a viable technical solution but life gets in the way. Key expertise, a key facility, or manufacturing capacity may not be available right then and it may be better to sacrifice the product instead of disrupting the pipeline. However, if the product development can be revived quickly (even at the same pipeline stage), then the knowledge can be re-used. The business case might estimate how many 'good' products don't make it through and estimate the value of developing a certain proportion of them. These arguments will also depend on whether the utilisation of staff and facilities is low enough not to disrupt other products' development.

KM in procurement

Just to be clear, purchasing is not what I'm talking about. Procurement is about identifying suppliers, negotiating appropriate contracts, managing supplier performance, and (in these outsourced times) will also involve choosing outsourcing partners. In a strange way, similar business case arguments can be used in procurement (or acquisition) and product development.

- **A better contract pipeline** – if suppliers that are not viable can be eliminated from tendering process earlier, then better contracts should result.
- **A faster contract pipeline** – means more corporate agility. This can mean the ability to negotiate new contracts, renegotiate imperfect contracts, and terminate obsolescent contracts without too much blowback. It can also shorten Time to Market and Time to Volume.
- **Better contracts** – good contracts placed with good suppliers who perform well and adapt to changing demand are going to enable better operational performance.
- **More contracts** – means more flexibility and faster responses to change, more options to manage risk – all these things have value and most organisations will have their own way of doing that.
- **Knowledge reuse** – lessons can be learned from good and bad negotiations and contracts, but also from particular sets of circumstances that may arise again. Reusing knowledge created as the organisation enters new markets or works with new suppliers will contribute to better, faster contracts to some degree.

Over the years I've done quite a few business cases and they've all been very different. It is always worth finding out what kind of arguments will succeed and the governance of change programmes already in place. In Western organisations ROI is very important, but in the Middle East social and political objectives are more important. I have set up as many arguments as I can substantiate for the different flavours of knowledge management and different areas of an organisation. When all is said and done, the judgments of the Programme Board on your rationale, your evidence, and your assumptions will be all important.

Chapter 3:
Using a knowledge audit to determine the ROI of knowledge management

By Tim Hawley, associate director of Arup

An introduction to using a knowledge audit

The purpose of a knowledge audit or K-Audit is to ascertain what knowledge exists in the organisation and what knowledge is needed to progress the organisation towards its strategic goals. In broadest terms this means a K-Audit determines what an organisation knows (and who knows what), what it does not know, what it needs to know, and what it should do to improve the management of knowledge. It should also assess how efficient and effective the organisational knowledge systems and processes are.

A K-Audit can therefore be an effective tool for enabling organisations to understand if they are getting a good return on investment on knowledge management, or it can determine how and where to get the best ROI in KM. A K-Audit does this by first establishing the baseline of knowledge management in an organisation and then determining the priority areas for development, with defined measurable outcomes, that can be used to inform the planning process, investment decisions, and the subsequent ROI.

Understanding the business drivers and strategy objectives define the destination point, but it is the current realities of the existing organisation, culture, and practice which defines the start. Establishing this start point is important for constructing an effective knowledge management strategy and plan by using the K-Audit to inform this process.

Designing the knowledge audit

The initial challenge with a knowledge audit is to keep it to an appropriate size – they can be highly intensive and comprehensive, drawing on a lot of resources, or they can be short and sharp, providing a good level of insight for the minimum effort. It will depend very much on the size and complexity of the organisation and the key objectives for the audit. So it is important to clearly define the goals of the knowledge audit, and to ensure the depth of scope, to ensure that time is focused on delivering the most value. Equally the breadth of scope should be set appropriately at either the enterprise, department, team, or process level.

The starting point for a K-Audit is an understanding of the business objectives and drivers for knowledge management in order to shape the purpose of the K-Audit. So that the focus is on checking alignment with knowledge needs and is grounded in the business realities.

In an ideal world every person in the organisation would be involved in a K-Audit, however given that this is likely impractical, the process will need to involve and engage a representative group of people across all disciplines, functions, and domains of activity across organisation. It is useful to segment the organisation appropriately for both ease of management of the process and also for comparison in the subsequent analysis. This should be done through workshops, focus groups, and the completion of structured reviews, either as a self-assessment or through interviews and work place discussions, asking people about the structure of knowledge within the domain in question.

Additionally surveys should also be considered as a good way to touch as many people as possible across the organisation, and can provide a rich source of material. It is important though to handle communications well, both to elicit responses and ensure expectations on outcomes are managed.

It is worth considering whether a pilot K-Audit should be done first to check whether the methodology and approaches are effective in eliciting the required information and that the people engaged by the process are receptive. It is also important to ensure that the communications are well managed, so that people understand the purpose and process that it is to use, what information is going to be collected, and how it will be used. It is also advisable to debrief people on the outcomes.

The K-Audit will map the knowledge base of the organisation, and can be expressed in a number of ways from reports and tables to creating a visual and conceptual framework, that makes sense of where the knowledge is within the relationship to complex processes, resources, and people. The K-Audit will look at where knowledge is stored, either explicitly in physical documents or held in ICT repositories, or tacitly in people's heads and across networks. Consideration is also given to how important the knowledge is, how easy to replace, how it is acquired, and who/where is it retained – a risk assessment scoring process can be used, for instance, considering 'criticality to the business' and 'ease of acquisition and retention'.

The value in completing a K-Audit is in identifying potential gaps and weaknesses, identifying knowledge flows, and for developing strategies to address issues and realise opportunities. These will form the basis of a plan that can be costed with values determined for the potential benefits that will form the basis of a business case, from which a return on investment can be measured. It is, therefore, important in the design of the audit to capture key metrics that can later be used to build a business case for investment, and then subsequently measuring the ROI. For instance, how much time is spent searching for knowledge? How costly are mistakes? What are the cost implications for lost knowledge? Etc.

K-Audit questions

The following is a list of typical questions that a knowledge audit will aim to investigate, which is comprehensive but not exhaustive, and the audit method needs to be tuned to the needs of the organisation:

- Is there an existing knowledge management strategy and if so is it aligned to the business and operating plans?
- Are the information and knowledge policies appropriate for enabling the knowledge needs of the organisation?
- Does the organisation 'know what it knows' and conversely 'know what it does not know'?
- Does the organisation know what the critical core knowledge is that enables it to operate effectively and compete?
- What is the expertise in the organisation, where is it located, and how can it be accessed?
- What and where are the existing knowledge assets (explicit, implicit, and tacit) and resources (location, form, and quality)?
- What is the status of the current knowledge management processes, and how do they enable knowledge capture, dissemination, use, and sharing.
- How standardised are the knowledge processes?
- Are the knowledge processes suitable for the business today, and to meet future aspirations?
- What knowledge management tools and techniques are used, and how widely?
- Are enabling systems and technologies deployed? Is their level of functionality appropriate for the purpose and what is the level of use?

- How does knowledge flow within the organisation?
- Where, or to whom, do people go to solve a problem?
- Are people able to get the knowledge they need when they need it?
- What is being done to tap in to potential knowledge sources?
- How do people collaborate together, sharing information, and knowledge?
- What are the current perceptions of knowledge management within the organisation and how does his vary?
- Do people 'reinvent the wheel' and 'duplicate effort'?
- How is decision making supported?
- How is knowledge security maintained and managed, are risks identified and mitigated?
- What are the organisational barriers to knowledge sharing?
- How are people incentivised and rewarded to share knowledge?
- How is knowledge retained within the organisation?
- Is value derived from knowledge management, are benefits known and tracked?

The output of a knowledge audit should give sufficient understanding and an awareness of the current state of knowledge management within the organisation, how aligned it is to the business strategy, what assets and resources are available, and what is required in the future. These outputs can be used as the basis for determining the plan and investment requirements to bridge the gap between the current state and the business needs.

K-Audit analysis

Through the information obtained from the K-Audit process it should be possible to determine the 'knowledge gap' between where the organisation currently is and where it needs to be, and critically what the benefit is in closing this gap in terms of hard measures. The analysis should provide insight from a number of key perspectives:

- Knowledge needs analysis – identification of what staff and the organisation need to know in order to meet the goals.
- Knowledge inventory analysis – a stock take on the current knowledge assets and resources, both explicit and tacit.

- Knowledge risk assessment – identification of the critical knowledge to the business and how vulnerable the organisation is to its loss.
- Knowledge process capability – an understanding on the status of the current KM processes, and how they enable knowledge capture, dissemination, use, and sharing.
- Knowledge network and flows – identification of how knowledge moves from where it's stored to where it's needed, and the barriers to effective flow.
- Knowledge enabling technology mapping – identification of how technology supports the identification, transfer, and retention of knowledge and information, and gaps in capability.
- Knowledge sharing cultural assessment – an understanding of how the organisational culture enables or inhibits the flow of knowledge and the level of KM maturity.

As well as providing this rich picture of how knowledge is managed within the organisation it should also be possible to determine what the benefits are from investing in KM and how they can be measured. The audit provides a baseline assessment of the current business and therefore a point from which improvement can be measured from in a variety of different aspects. The K-Audit should provide a rich source of information around organisational and operational efficiency that should allow some quantitative figures to be established, so that a financial benefits case can be derived with supporting evidence. This knowledge can also be used to help prioritise the areas that will provide the most benefits within the knowledge management improvement plan.

Determining the business benefits

Business benefits from KM can fall into two broad categories, either as 'hard' (tangible benefits) or as 'soft' (intangible benefits). The 'hard' tangible benefits are obviously ideal as they can be easily measured and can be used to derive and demonstrate performance improvement. The 'soft' intangible benefits are by definition harder to quantify, but their benefits to the organisation should not be underestimated as they can be an important enabler and even a competitive differentiator.

Hard benefit examples:

- Reduced duplication costs;
- Reduced re-work/corrective costs;

- Increased productivity;
- Reduced transaction processing times;
- Cost avoidance;
- Reduced development cycles; and
- Reduced time spent accessing knowledge and information.

Soft benefits examples:

- Employee satisfaction;
- Improved customer relationships;
- Retention of critical knowledge;
- Increased organisational flexibility;
- Development of wider organisational capabilities; and
- A more collaborative culture.

However, a key challenge is that knowledge management activities often only indirectly impact business outcomes. As knowledge management activities are generally social processes based on the creation and integration of knowledge, organisational engagement, and learning. Their direct effect is on business processes, the transactional flow of the operational and functional activities of the business along its value chain. It is the performance of the business processes, measured by normal business metrics, which effect business outcomes.

However, understanding the influence of these indirect relationships can help determine how the return on investment in knowledge management can result in improved business outcomes. Therefore this relationship can be determined with a benefits map between knowledge management activities or initiatives and the required business outcomes, which can also in turn be linked to the business strategic objectives.

A benefits map provides a 'clear line of sight' between the KM initiative deliverables or outputs and the business benefits. It is usually set out in a visual form of interlinked boxes, starting on the left hand side by identifying all the KM project activities and their outputs, then moving to the right through desired business outcomes towards the strategic objectives. The first step is to categorise the different types of benefits and how the organisation will measures their value. Ideally, existing performance measures should be used as the approaches for collecting are already in place. The K-Audit will have provided the opportunity to

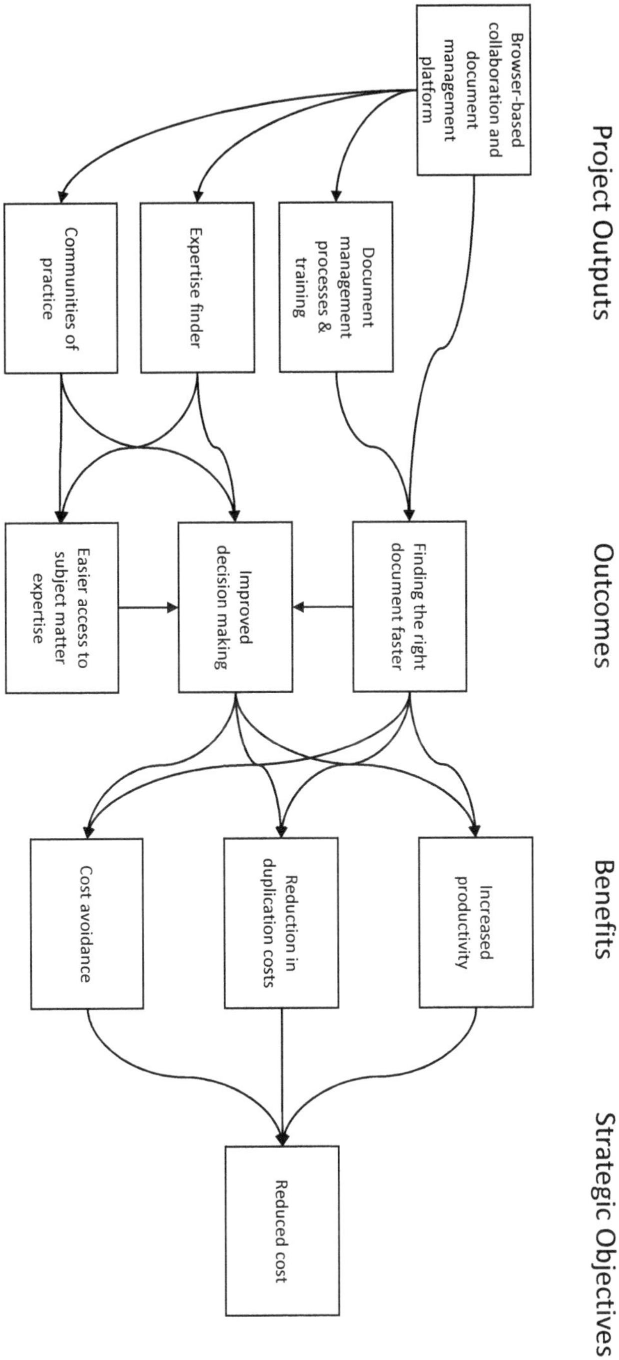
Project Outputs
Outcomes
Benefits
Strategic Objectives
Browser-based collaboration and document management platform
Document management processes & training
Expertise finder
Communities of practice
Finding the right document faster
Improved decision making
Easier access to subject matter expertise
Increased productivity
Reduction in duplication costs
Cost avoidance
Reduced cost

establish baseline performance metrics that future benefit delivery can be measured from.

The benefits mapping boxes should set out the required outcomes required to realise the benefits, and define the project outputs needed to enable these outcomes. The boxes should be linked with arrows indicating the flow of capability and benefits, and their interdependences, communicating a visualisation of how the project will deliver business benefits. A very simple benefits map model is shown in figure 1 on page 25.

With a baseline set of measures from the K-Audit and a prioritised view of where the benefits will be derived from KM mapped against the benefits. It should be possible to establish a set of measures that show how KM is supporting the delivery of business outcomes, where KM is adding value and also where it is not. In short this process should provide the basis for measuring the ROI of KM.

Chapter 4:
Application of artificial intelligence to build value in organisational knowledge and assist ROI

By James Loft, chief executive officer at Matter AI

Artificial intelligence is here, it's been here for a while and it is not going away, although contrary to popular belief the robots are not going to take over any time soon.

In this chapter I hope to outline a view of the current AI landscape and some of the possible ways in which it can be used for adding value in the knowledge management space. Additionally, how it can support the return on investment for knowledge work and potentially support success where the financial outlay is initially small but the potential benefit, both financial and organisational, is great.

I will give a view of the marketplace and explain some of the ways in which AI can support knowledge in organisation, touch on what makes an AI business case, and explore some of the successes that are already in the world to see. AI is not only the tool of the wealthy organisation nor is it the playground of financial services, as is often perceived. In the work we do, using our knowledge and expertise to support businesses through their AI journey, it is clear that no industry is taking the lead in the use of AI technologies.

On an average week my consulting team will speak with people across various industries, for example, law, retail, travel, media, utilities, telecoms, tax and accounting, advisory, and insurance – all of whom are interested in understanding the various technologies and tools available. However, as there is no clear space or sector for AI it cannot have a clear and immediate value.

In order to best discuss the possible success factors and benefits of AI, especially in the knowledge space, it is important to be explicit from the start as to what we specifically mean by AI.

In the wider sense it is not a new term or theory, nor is the practice new as mechanical calculation machines having been in existence since the middle ages, completing tasks previously required to be completed by humans. Systems such as ABS breaking have been doing the same in cars for many years since being launched in the aviation industry.

The categorisation of AI is potentially one of the most important elements for there to be a success in the fields where it currently has active work being developed. This in part is a lot to do with the language and acceptance of new technologies and advances in AI. Common terms used both to describe and discredit AI include the polarities of Weak (generally described as what we currently have) and Strong, which is usually described as a mildly dystopian based robot figure that is cleverer than the humans it interacts with and will eventually take over.

The issue with this is that these polarities are not helpful, for the latter is not necessarily a progression of the former and it should not be used as the scale to view the possibilities. For example, a general AI that knows everything and acts autonomously is not the right point to aim our efforts at achieving, instead a combined, practical, or applied goal is a more realistic one that is not only achievable but useful, and supports the challenges that people and organisations face today and in the near future.

There is an existing dilemma or challenge with AI that means humans have a tendency to downgrade it to not being AI or being less than AI as soon as it has success. This is something that is reflected in the general opinion around AI and is often the journalistic approach that is adopted – as it is easier to discredit the success of AI than to explain the value. This makes the acceptance of the technology or willingness to try new approaches a hard one to achieve, especially within board rooms, where the existing opportunity to follow well-trodden and linear paths is tough to deviate from. Although the challenges are not the same, I believe that the outcome reflects some of the challenges knowledge management led initiatives face in organisations today. However, one of the variances is that AI has the opportunity to be implemented in a far more agile and iterative way. With the right support and engagement in an organisation AI can be a catalyst for its own success and increase the value of the knowledge in an organisation in general. In summary, AI can act to both enhance a business and support the knowledge maturity of the business at the same time.

The current marketplace

The current AI marketplace is a busy environment with new and established tools and platforms appearing regularly. From a technical perspective, there is such a variety in not only the companies but also in the tools and services available that this environment is well established and invested in but not yet formed into a clearly navigable marketplace.

Current platforms and tools span from call centre specific systems, such as that from Digital Genius (https://digitalgenius.com), which automates interactions with customers using machine learning to tackle high volume common questions based on previous behaviours and responses. There are organisations such as Re-Infer (https://reinfer.io) that can give more meaning and value to the information and feedback given by customers in an hour, compared to what a human data team could acquire in a week. Then there are complex cognitive reasoning tools like Rainbird (http://rainbird.ai) that will make complex decisions such as tax or financial advice decisions for colleagues or customers, and then go on to explain why that decision was made. These few examples are the current tools that are set to have big impacts on our lives. However, there are many others with the funding and support to grow and become equally useful tools.

These additional tools are currently being deployed in a number of environments within many different organisations. They overlap in their mission but tackle very different business challenges in continually unique ways that give them value over each other. Dependant on the situation that they are being applied within, all can work together in unison and add real value to a business and solve these challenges. These examples are advanced and specific tools; all are in some way supported by, or work in harmony with, the technologies being created by the larger organisations in this industry. For example, IBM, Google, Facebook, and Microsoft, all of which (and especially IBM with Watson) have major and powerful tools in the AI marketplace.

Both IBM and Google have concentrated their focus on the medical space, whilst other large organisations have put a lot of time and effort into the driverless car advancements, which will clearly be a step change in technology that many of us won't have seen in our lifetimes. However, these could also drown out a lot of the more beneficial practical applications of AI through the size of such change and possible impacts. All of these options, either through the larger organisations or smaller specific technologies, are accessible to companies to use and affordable to implement and run.

Benefit themes

There are some AI benefits that directly relate to organisational knowledge, or to be specific, information that has the potential to become organisational knowledge with the right technological support. These examples demonstrate the impact AI can have on the information in order for it to add value to the organisation. They are covered within four main and obvious themes however, these are not the only areas where this kind of technology can provide support.

Uniformity

One of the challenges laid at the door of AI is that it lacks empathy, and could therefore never communicate as well as a human. This is true in as much as a computer cannot have its own feelings that is expresses. However, AI tools can identify human emotions, behaviours, and even in some examples identify biometric patterns to allow it to make suggestions based on previous patterns and written knowledge, to propose the right way of dealing with a situation. It provides a logical, emotional response although it doesn't have one of its own. So although it is widely acknowledged that artificial emotional intelligence is within that "strong" camp for the future, organisations can benefit from a uniformed output that can provide an emotional consistency to organisations in dealing with customers.

This is well demonstrated in the call centre environment; it can be a tool to take all of the available policies and procedures for a product or service and offer an altered script or path to an agent, based on the topic being discussed or on some emotional or biometric triggers picked up during the call. This is the same human behaviour that an agent is employed to have, but removes the risk of the agent having had three bad calls in a row, and without them needing to know the potential paths to take within the company's procedures. Essentially it gives the entire knowledge of the business to the call agent to enable them to avoid problems and increase the likelihood of first point resolution. This is achieved by levelling the playing field across team members and making the entire team as equipped as the best team member on any given day. If automated script writing is also employed then there could be an opportunity to save conversations that would otherwise have ended in a second call or a complaint being raised.

Knowledge banks

Most organisations, especially those that have seen rapid growth over a short period of time, have a large collection of information relating to the products offered, their policies within which they work, and the procedures for dealing with issues or questions from customers.

This is often increased in the environment where success has been achieved and the organisation has grown its customer base or product offering to a size that dwarfs its previous review or set up. These systems have been added to time and time again in order to include all of the new information.

Team members that deal with customers have often created localised 'short cuts' or improvements to the how things are done. These may be unrecorded beyond written notes or sit on intranet sites where colleagues discuss their challenges and successes. This sign of success is linked to organisational growth but it often leads to a process based or formalised way of updating information. Which sadly means there is always something new for people to know and interpret the importance of themselves.

Where AI can add value in this space is that it loves to read (this is why IBM has had the success it has in the field of oncology with Watson) and makes connections from the information it has taken on board.

Therefore, a system that has read and interpreted everything can apply all of this to its consumed knowledge of the regulation or law within which the business sits. With the interpretation of human language it is possible to instantly return an edited version of the information it has read with the correct relevance. This is a tool worth plugging your teams into to enhance their service. It allows for conversation and relationships to return to being the primary element in the customer interaction and for them to be offered the latest personalised information or advice. Meaning shorter and better conversations, more first level resolution to questions and challenges, and a reduction in the possibility of incorrect or out of date information being shared with customers.

Chatbots and the simplified lens of the complex

Chatbots are easily dismissed as not being AI, and indeed a chat interface itself is not. However, what they are is a more human and user aligned way of communicating. The AI addition to a chatbot not only allows for a conversation to be held automatically in a coherent language that humans understand and can relate to, but it also gives it the opportunity to be a live service in hours otherwise unachievable with humans. It also allows for conversations to be held over a period of time in an asynchronous way that is far more aligned to the text and messenger based behaviours increasingly demonstrated by more and more users.

There is a secondary benefit to organisations that allows for the conversation to be constant and never really stop. Further value chatbots achieve is the ability to use the technology to assist in the simplification of complex information, turning information into having immediate and powerful value to its receiver. This approach provides the opportunity for a change in how and when services are opened out to customers. It has both a reduction in the need for manual intervention but also offers the opportunity to reduce the agent hours required. This doesn't replace the agents all together, but it does move the model towards less transactional and more knowledge based teams, that can be both smaller and remote, but capable of far more unique support.

Decision making

The most complex example of AI in organisations currently are the decision elements for AI which are more complex and, as a result, should in theory add a greater level of value. Current examples of AI based decision systems include an approach to complex advice such as legal or tax advice, although it is not trying to compete with the senior accountants and lawyers. Yet a large proportion of the decision systems which use an approach that looks to prove itself wrong are being used. This includes drafting contracts, giving tax advice usually completed by juniors, researching cases, and giving complex answers to questions that have a vast number of variations in their make-up. The key success factor in this situation is that they will give an answer and then proceed to highlight and identify exactly why they gave that answer and what their thought process was. This is a huge auditory step forward and also demonstrates yet again a shift in organisation knowledge based on the way the tool is built and the parameters it is taught, rather than a number of individuals making situation based decisions.

The importance of design

AI has a natural kin in service design and agile build delivery methods, therefore an iterative approach is both possible and reasonable to achieve. As a result, AI technologies can be tested or built on lower budgets and easily scaled to meet need or demand. Service Design helps develop the concept of a minimal viable proposition as an initial creation, this being a topic or part of a service that can demonstrate an immediate benefit on a small scale.

Because AI is still considered to be exploratory, projects are often required to start on a small scale and are often aligned to innovation or process improvement budgets, rather than IT budgets.

Even large organisations such as those in banking who have invested more than most industries in AI are still in the trial phases, although there is great support. They will initially try to review the potential of the technologies on a low level often choosing to tackle elements where there is an existing but not regulatory bound challenge. They tend to reflect a desire to demystify a set of product detail or to remove a manual and heavily repeated element of an existing process, such as changing address. The addition of value here is partly what makes the current approach easily referred to as actionable or applied, as they are not setting out to solve knowledge sharing or completely change the way products are offered. They are starting with a single product, a single set of customers, and a single set of colleagues; they are then using a proof of concept approach to establish a working model that adds value before being expanded out from that point. This allows for small budgets to be used to demonstrate need and desire in an effective and positive way, which means that knowledge teams can take an ownership over the implementation of technology that adds value to the 'organisational brain', rather than working with what is made available or laid out by technologists.

AI and business cases

As is common in knowledge management projects where the value from AI systems is often not a stand-alone saving and may need to be worked into a larger business case or be treated as an enabler, although if volume is applied a business case becomes easier.

In a call centre, for example, where the knowledge system is consumed by AI and webchat is semi-automated savings would come in a number of separate formats such as:

- Calls would be quicker resulting in an overall increase in the number of calls taken and at scale a reduction in call handlers for specific topics;
- First point of contact resolution will increase, therefore the same reduction in call time will occur. The need to hand off to specialist teams will reduce and customer satisfaction would increase; and
- The availability of a semi-automated webchat will relieve the need for the support levels manually provided within agent hours and greater levels of basic support outside of them, increasing the 'self-serve' opportunities and generally reducing the cost to serve over time.

All of this is underpinned by an increase in accuracy that can remove repeat or secondary contact from customers whilst constantly learning, improving, and suggesting the next step. Overall this gives a compelling case for spending against a number of key and achievable goals, leading to far more traditional and tangible benefits as progression happens – if they are the kind of expectations specific organisations consider to be needed.

Value can also be demonstrated by AI in how it gives a new value to the organisation's knowledge through the opportunity to be used and continuously improved by interactions with customers and colleagues, thus enhancing itself through precise updates with a new centralised control. This means that product team changes, risk variations, and regulatory changes can all be easily carried out at the information level and that the responsibility for knowing new elements is moved away from specific individuals or teams. Therefore, the system provides the organisation with the opportunity to have 'live' information maintained to a higher standard than has been possible previously. It can help to avoid inaccuracies in its application as it offers the latest and most specific options and solutions. It can ask users questions in line with policy detail to ensure the right information is gathered to get the best possible response.

As a result of this, there is an underlying opportunity to turn colleagues into relationship leads again, something many of them were recruited for having demonstrated their capabilities in, and improves the general customer satisfaction and reduces churn. In the financial services environment, this has created an opportunity to start seeing an ROI against the risk pot for concerns over miss-selling or product challenges, as it can demonstrate the auditable approach it took to make a recommendation.

AI adding extra value to knowledge

AI has the capabilities to turn information previously perceived within marketing ownership, not organisational knowledge, often captured through survey, social media, and direct contact information into not just manageable but actionable knowledge. It does this in a fraction of the time and free of bias compared to the previous human teams who read and interpreted the same information. Therefore, suddenly what was previously a large amount of data, often unexplored due to its volume, is now a collection of themes that can be sectioned off to the individuals for whom they have the most value.

For example, in a company that provides goods packaged and posted in the Christmas rush. Not only do they know that customers have had issues, but they can highlight to their technical teams that people within a specific geography, on a specific device, and at a specific time of the day are reporting similar negative issues on the checkout button.

Traditional analytics would likely have highlighted a 'drop off' in a specific space if they were being carefully watched, but would not have been able to flag the verbatim information to a specific team to resolve the issue. This same actionable output can be applied to product teams, project teams, senior managers, and on the whole can give a better insight into the customer perceptions and challenges than the more traditional approaches such as NPS could ever achieve.

Summary

AI has been around in various guises for a number of years, it has a journey to go on that it will eventually achieve. However, there are a myriad of value offerings it can add to people and organisations now. Most of which are in some way linked to the value of the organisations knowledge and how it is balanced between centralised and remote user control. AI can also uniform and enhance the knowledge offering for businesses and can be used as a catalyst for the business cases of knowledge projects.

Chapter 5:
Measurement of KM projects – A practical guide for busy people

By Hélène Russell, founder of TheKnowledgeBusiness

This chapter looks at the measurement of knowledge projects and activities in a simple, practical way, with the aim of helping busy individuals understand whether their various knowledge management projects and activities are having a positive effect and are value for money in a general sense. Be forewarned: the benefits of KM are often intangible and the way that KM affects tangibles can be complex, so measurement is difficult. That doesn't, however, mean that you can't approximate an answer which is useful within a business setting.

The value and difficulty of measuring

There are many different ways that knowledge artifacts and flows can benefit organisations (see Figure 1).

Figure 1: The benefits of knowledge management

Measuring the numbers of knowledge artifacts or activities is not usually difficult. You could probably easily find out how many articles you have in your organisation's database or how many training meetings took place last month. The difficulty lies in understanding how those artifacts/activities are acting on your organisation to help or hinder it in its goals, understanding the quality of those knowledge artifacts/activities, and whether they provide a good return on investment.

When considering the effect of artifacts and activities, there are usually many complex factors at play. X does not simply cause Y. The effects of a single knowledge project are intricately entwined with other business systems, affected by serendipitous events, and events outside the organisation's control.

For example, a lawyer is mulling over a complex issue and is planning to look at the firm's knowledge bank before drafting a complex document. He decides to get a coffee first. Whilst making his coffee he chats to another lawyer and discovers that she has recently dealt with the same issue, researched it intensively, and found a neat solution which her client was delighted with. This is clearly a successful knowledge activity/interaction: the first lawyer gets the right information and knowledge quickly and easily, and finds a solution which is likely to please his client. What, however, would be measured and what would this interaction tell us about this law firm's KM systems? Nothing would be recorded in any database viewing or download figures and it may not be recalled by either lawyer during an annual knowledge survey or discussion about culture and networks. Is this a success for the knowledge-sharing culture, a failure of the knowledge database, neither, or both?

Similarly when lawyers or other professionals are trying to understand whether it is more cost-effective to work in one way rather than another, perhaps deciding whether to impose a particular workflow or checklist, this may have a more complicated result than a simple change in billings or profits (see Figure 2). There could be lower chargeable hours per matter and lower billing levels in the short term, but, in the long term, higher quality advice, higher customer satisfaction, lower professional negligence claims, lower attrition rates, and more matters undertaken or higher profit fixed fees.

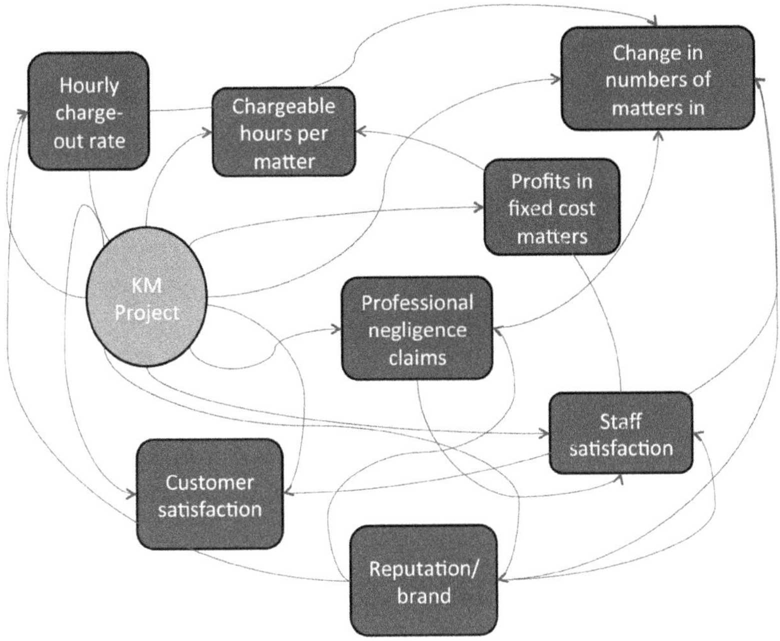

Figure 2: The effects of knowledge management projects

How well KM activities work in an organisation depends greatly on its culture, history, and the dedication of the individuals involved – and factors outside the organisation's control can have a significant effect.

Although it is undoubtedly difficult to value 'knowledge' and knowledge activities and systems, the pragmatic truth is that those who run organisations need to understand what return on investment they will get for their spending on KM, which projects or schemes ought to be rolled out more widely, and which projects or activities should be changed.

Where to start with KM measurement

I recommend, when planning your measurement system, you use the following process (see Figure 3 for the full process):

1. **Why** – understand your **purpose** in measuring;
2. **Who** – understand your **audience** for the measurement; and
3. **How** – understand the **practicalities** of measuring for an accurate result.

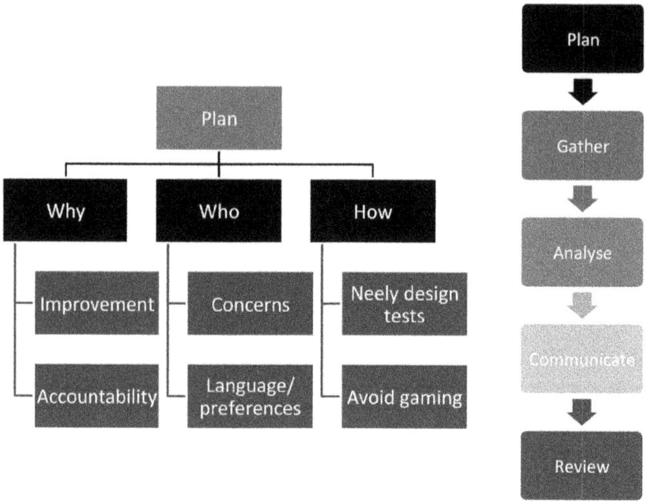

Figure 3: How to create and use measurement systems in KM

Also keep in mind these two truisms:

What is measured gets managed.

What is measured within a business tends to get noticed and improved. Things that aren't measured often languish on the 'to do' pile.

You get what you measure.

Measurement itself can have unexpected and negative results, with employees focusing on improving figures themselves rather than the business case behind those measurements.

Why: Understanding your purpose

Your first task is to understand your purpose:

- Why do you need this measurement?
- What is the business benefit of knowing this answer?
- What are you going to do with the results?

You need to take the appropriate level of measurements to inform and support your decision-making and action. There is no point in measurement for measurement's sake and too many measurements can be counterproductive as they can create confusion. If you can't take action based on the measurement in relation to that KM project or activity, don't waste time and money on that aspect (unless you are gathering evidence for a known future action).

If you are unsure whether your measurement is actionable, ask yourself whether you want the measurement to go up, down, or stay flat. If you don't know which way you want the measurement to go, or don't know what you will do in each situation, the measurement is not actionable and you need to think again.

Common reasons for measuring KM activities are:

- Improvement/quality; and
- Judgment/accountability.

For example, most KMers will be measuring to find out:

- If their actions are adding value to the organisation;
- If an investment in a particular project or KM activity is value for money;
- Whether or not a particular implementation is on track, a particular approach is working, and to identify gaps in their approach;
- Whether they should expand a pilot KM project or shelve it;
- Where a project doesn't appear to be working, whether that is an inherent problem and that project is unlikely ever to work within their organisation, or whether it can be put back-on-track with a few tweaks;
- What their users/stakeholders natural modes of working are, in order to design KM activities which suit them and will be adopted easily;
- Whether their stakeholders are fulfilling their part of the KM-bargain or not, and if not, how the system can be adapted to encourage more participation; and
- To identify the key barriers to engagement.

Your 'purpose' for measuring will drive the development of your measurement systems.

Given how difficult it is to understand the effect of KM activities and projects on business outcomes (see Figure 2), I recommend that you take a balance of measurements. The complexity of your measurement system will depend upon the size and nature of the project and budget, but I recommend that, even for a small project, you at least include qualitative and quantitative, and leading and lagging elements. Whether you measure across all four perspectives of the Balanced Scorecard depends on the project and its budget. Too many measurements are as unhelpful as too few.

The Balanced Scorecard

The Balanced Scorecard was first proposed by Kaplan and Norton in 1992[1] and updated in 2000[2] and is one of the most influential business ideas in relation to business drivers over the last 75 years. They understood that traditional financial accounting measures, such as earnings per share and return on investment can give misleading signals and negatively affect a business's ability to innovate and improve continuously.[3]

The Balanced Scorecard emphasises a simple but balanced perspective, using a handful of hard and soft measures and leading and lagging indicators, built around four key areas, asking four basic questions:

1. How do customers see us? (customer perspective);
2. What must we excel at? (internal business perspective);
3. Can we continue to improve and create value? (innovation, knowledge, and learning perspective); and
4. How do we look to shareholders and financially? (financial stewardship perspective)

It aims to act like 'dials in a cock pit' so that managers can take in complex information from all four perspectives at a glance, and, ensuring that improvements in one area (say, financial) are not at the expense of other areas (say, customer perspective or innovation/learning), keep the organisation on track against its strategy. It is the 'hands down favourite' of Dr Melissie Rumizen, author of 'The Complete Idiot's Guide to Knowledge Management'.[4]

The Balanced Scorecard also blends 'looking back' and 'looking forward' to keep organisations on track. It is fairly easy to measure what has happened in the past. This will tell you whether what you have done in the past has worked or not, but it won't tell you whether what you are currently doing will be a success.

'Looking back' measures are 'lagging indicators' and are output measures, such as changes to profitability, and tell you what has already happened.

'Looking forward' measures are 'leading indicators' and are input measures, such as the ongoing costs (of staff, of IT) and activity measures such as level of participation (web page views, amount of activity on a wiki), and give you 'early warning' of what might happen.

'Leading' and 'lagging' are not absolute notions. Leading is upstream in a work process. Lagging is downstream in the same process. A particular measurement can be upstream when measuring one aspect and downstream for another, and some measurements can be difficult to categorise. Both leading and lagging factors can be quantitative or qualitative.

For example, if you work in a knowledge intensive firm and you would like to trial a change to a training and learning programme by swapping from in-person training lunches based on lectures, to online videos and quizzes, you could wait until the programme has run its course, had a positive or negative effect on the knowledgeability of your staff and led to a measurable change in numbers of clients and profitability, or you could take leading measurements to give you early warning if the programme isn't working. Leading measurements in this case could include the numbers of people taking, finishing, or passing the online courses. If the numbers of people wanting to start the course drops, perhaps word has spread that people do not feel the courses are worth investing time in? If people are keen to start and finish, but fail the quizzes, you will get an early warning that something is not right with the content or delivery of the knowledge.

Who: Understanding the audience for the measurement

It doesn't really matter how sound your data[5] is, if you cannot communicate the results in a way that is persuasive for those who need to take action.

Common audiences for the measurement are:

- Those running KM activities or projects;
- Users, stakeholders, or communities your KM activities/projects serve; and
- Managers and directors at various levels in the organisation and those who allocate resources.

Once you've clarified your audience, you need to ask yourself:

For the purpose I've identified, what does this audience 'care' about?

Concentrate on the measurements or KPIs within the four Balanced Scorecard perspectives that your audience cares particularly about. You can look at financial stewardship in a number of ways, but your senior managers probably have a favourite measurement they always take notice of. No matter how great you think your measurements are, if they don't persuade those who need to take action, they haven't fulfilled their purpose.

If you are uncertain about a particular audience's preferences, ask them. This isn't a matter of 'sexing up' data to mislead. It is about avoiding wasting time measuring one aspect when a different but similar one would have a more persuasive effect on that audience. Even if their preferred measurement isn't the perfect one in your opinion, still use it. It has the benefit of being established and authoritative to your audience. If you really can't use it, explain how your measurements link to it.

For example, you are measuring to demonstrate that a particular discrete KM project is making a significant difference to profitability and ought to be rolled out more widely and your audience is senior managers.

Ask yourself:

- What do those senior managers care about? What keeps them up at night?
- What data have they previously taken notice of?
- What 'language' do they listen to and speak?

The senior managers may worry about profitability, levels of innovation when new competitors enter their market, or key staff attrition after a merger, depending on what is happening in the organisation at the time. They may be mainly from a financial background and take notice of short term share price changes or profit per equity partner. They may care most about market position and client satisfaction surveys. They may care greatly about efficiency and effectiveness.

Alternatively, if you are using a measurement to help you understand whether a smaller KM project appears to be a good use of your own limited time, you may focus on measurements which you personally find compelling. For example, you think a project relating to serendipitous conversation will improve trusting networks and person-to-person knowledge sharing. It isn't a complex, expensive, unpopular, or onerous project, so you may want to minimise the cost of measurement and focus on a simple one-off qualitative measurement, such as a survey or focus group. Once you have satisfied yourself that the project appears to be working and is worth rolling out further, you may widen measurements across the four Balanced Scorecard perspectives to ensure that there are no unanticipated negative results which could steer your organisation off course and which will include measurements meaningful for the new audience, who may not be persuaded by a focus group discussion, but may be persuaded by a reduction in early notification of potential professional negligence claims or an increase in client satisfaction measurements in relation to knowledgeability of staff.

Try also, where possible, to gather stories which illustrate your data, as well as the data itself. Whilst an increase in general client satisfaction measurements may be compelling, hearing the audio file of the actual interview with a client expressing in their own words how the knowledgeability of staff persuaded them to place more orders is even more compelling.

How: Deciding on the practicalities of measurement

Once you are clear on the purpose of your measurement and its audience, you will need to decide on the practicalities. Your measurements should be reliable and valid and, for larger projects, you should spell out your methodology in detail.

You need to be clear about:

- What measurements are you going to take? How you are going to take them?
- Who will collect the data?
- How, when, and how often will they collect it?

You will also need to consider how much you can afford to spend on measurement. Some measurements will be collected in any event, so are low in cost (although don't forget that you'll still need to analyse the results) and some will cost money to arrange, collect, and analyse. The nature of your KM project and its potential to affect your organisation will determine your budget for measurement.

As you are only measuring to take action in relation to your KM project and activities, you need to have a trustworthy baseline from which to note changes. You must also ensure you take the same measurements in the same way before and after the change for the results to be reliable ('comparing apples with apples').

A balance of measurements (using qualitative and quantitative, leading and lagging, across the four facets of the Balanced Scorecard) can get us closer to understanding what is happening as a result of our activities and overcoming the difficulties outlined at page 38. It will also help us to even out any gaming[6] (see page 47).

User surveys are extremely valuable for qualitative research, but can't be used too often because of user-fatigue. Surveys can include both qualitative and quantitative elements and can focus on one project or activity or combine questions about a number of them. Where you would like to distil an opinion into an easily comparable figure, I recommend using a Likert Scale (where your respondents rate their response from 1 to 5, 1 being 'strongly disagree' and 5 being 'strongly agree'). There is more advice on how to write a good survey at Annex 4. Informal discussions are just as important as formal soundings, so also get to know what people think by talking to them.

At this point, I recommend that you take a moment to read and understand the ten measurement design tests (Figure 4 and Annex 2) described by Professor Andrew Neely, head of the Institute of Manufacturing at Cambridge and expert in designing KPIs and measuring business performance.

Neely Design Tests

1. The truth test
2. The focus test
3. The relevancy test
4. The consistency test
5. The access test
6. The clarity test
7. The so-what test
8. The timeliness test
9. The cost test
10. The gaming test

Figure 4: The Neely Design Tests

Whilst not all KM projects will be sufficiently large to warrant measurements which fulfil all these design tests, they are a great checklist to ensure that:

- You measure only what is necessary and relevant at the time that it is needed;
- Your measurements are the easiest and cheapest measurements to take, and remain consistent whoever gathers the data; and
- You continue to measure only what you set out to measure.

You need to understand what is truly important to the firm to ensure that you concentrate on the right aspects. Once you have your data, remember that all measurements are not equal in value: 'non-chargeable time saved' within a law firm is unlikely to be more important than quality, firm reputation or new business won, unless the changes are sizeable.

Unintended consequences and 'gaming'

Measurement systems can cause distortions and unexpected consequences, particularly where they are linked to performance. These distortions can be conscious or subconscious, as people change their behaviour to meet the targets set for them or the measurement systems applied to them.

There are numerous examples of unintended consequences to measurement systems in everyday life: teachers teaching to the test for SATs, not to benefit pupils' needs, but to improve their school's ranking or avoid criticism by Ofsted; GPs refusing to book patients in for appointments at all, even when patients are happy to wait, so as not to breach government rules about patients waiting 48 hours for an appointment.

People are nearly always more intelligent than systems. Your users and particularly your subject matter experts are likely to spot any weaknesses in your measurement systems and work out how to 'game' the results that affect them. Quantitative measurements are particularly susceptible to gaming and so should always be balanced with qualitative measurements.

For example, in a law firm, you decide to measure numbers of submissions to a KM database as part of your measurements to try to understand the value of that database and the knowledge-sharing attitude of your lawyers. You wish to promote knowledge sharing, so you also reward this, perhaps by noting it during annual appraisals. You find an annual spike of submissions shortly before performance reviews. Of course this is not a problem if the quality is good, although it would be easier to manage if submissions were spread out throughout the year, but in truth, quality is unlikely to be good if 'box ticking' is the motivator. The firm 'gets what it measures', in that it emphasises other aspects of profitability all year, then switches to 'softer' aspects at appraisal time.

Gaming can be minimised by approaching measurement using a number of different angles and by keeping an eye out for unusual results or improvements in quantitative results which don't reflect an improvement in quality, or are not matched by qualitative comments.

Analysis of data

As part of this practical guide, I won't be delving deeply into statistical analysis. My own experience has been that, in most cases, only simple tools are needed. You are primarily looking for relationships and trends, i.e. when X happens, what happens to Y? You will usually just need percentages, averages, ratios, and divergence from the mean/median/mode. If the picture you uncover appears to be more complex, I recommend you tap into your network for help from someone with the right data analysis skills.

Reporting results

No matter how carefully you collate your data, you will need to communicate your results in a compelling way for it to be persuasive.

- Engage with your audience's needs and wants;
- Give enough context so that people can understand the results;
- Include the human face to the figures – a story or anecdote will have impact on your audience; and
- Decide where and how to publicise the results. If you plan to release the results on to the intranet, who will see it? Do you want all the results available to everyone, or do you want a detailed version for the Executive Board and a slimmed down version for the whole organisation? What state of mind will your audience be in when they receive your results? How can you maximise their understanding?

Updating your measurements

As you gain experience in measuring your KM projects/activities, you will need to revise and update your measurement system. You may find that some of the goals (the 'Why', see page 40) need more work. Your organisation will also grow, adapt to different customers, change its IT systems etc. You will need to identify any overlapping measurements and simplify them. You will need to replace measurements that are proving to be unhelpful, or those that have become too costly to justify. You will learn which measurements work particularly well with which audiences. You will need to keep a delicate balance between keeping measurements the same (so you can identify trends over time, measuring apples against apples) and adapting to new circumstances, and simplifying and focusing your measurements.

I recommend that you revisit your measurements and the Neely design tests at suitable intervals, perhaps annually, and adapt the measurements as appropriate.

Summary

Use Figure 2 to help you plan and implement your measurement systems.

1. Define the business objectives of measurement and understand what success will look like;
2. Identify those being measured and the audience for the results – each stakeholder views KM and defines success differently;
3. Decide what data will be collected and how. Use Neely's measurement design tests to ensure your measurements are appropriate;
4. Analyse and communicate the measures in the language of your audience;
5. Take action in relation to business objectives based on the results;
6. Review your combination of measures to ensure the right balance of quantitative and qualitative, leading and lagging measurements, and adjust as your goals develop;
7. Keep under review unexpected consequences and 'gaming' the system of measurement; and
8. Don't measure everything – focus on what's important.

Annex 1

The big list of potential ways to measure KM systems

Quantitative:

1. System user statistics;
2. Hits on a webpage;
3. Load times of web pages;
4. Dwell times (how long a user stays on a page);
5. Numbers of unique users;
6. Repeat visitors to a page;
7. Usage of externally provided KM;
8. Percentage of total employees using a system;
9. Uses of a precedent/the precedent database;
10. Number of contributions to knowledge database;
11. Number of questions asked on a discussion forum;
12. Frequency of updates by users;

13. Numbers of active community members;
14. Frequency of AAR meetings;
15. Number of calls to Information Services professionals;
16. Number of queries raised and responded to;
17. Time taken to respond to queries;
18. Number of people trained in KM;
19. Number of KM champions or sponsors;
20. Training events prepared/attended;
21. Length of time devoted to certain activities (e.g. preparing tenders or client seminars);
22. Non-chargeable time recorded;
23. Speed of document production;
24. Time to create new knowledge;
25. Number of repeat complaints;
26. Professional indemnity insurance claims;
27. Number of identified experts;
28. Number of people active in Communities of Practice (CoPs);
29. Number of new employees;
30. Level of staff retention;
31. Retention of key staff;
32. Number of clients lost to leaving staff;
33. Number of knowledge debriefs;
34. Number of knowledge stories;
35. Invitations to speak at conferences/seminars, etc;
36. Number of publications in relevant literature;
37. Number of contacts with knowledge institutes;
38. Benchmarking against suppliers, customers, and peer businesses;
39. KM budget availability;
40. Proportion of employees making new idea suggestions;

41. Time to develop new ideas;
42. Ratio of new ideas generated to new ideas implemented;
43. Percentage of sales earned with new knowledge;
44. Savings by knowledge re-use;
45. Support staff cost reductions;
46. Reduction in cost of quality;
47. Information maintenance costs;
48. KM IT tool outage levels;
49. Level of leverage within a department;
50. Percentage of profit from fixed fee work;
51. Utilisation level within a department;
52. Realisation levels within a department;
53. Change in ranking in expert Directories (such as Legal 500 or Chambers); and
54. Level of understanding of KM within business plan/KM vision.

Qualitative:
Could be measured by surveys (of users, of support staff, of supervisors), focus groups, consultations etc.

1. Ease of access;
2. Quality of document production (that is, fewer mistakes);
3. Ease of location of an expert;
4. User (both user and support staff) satisfaction;
5. Confidence in the systems (success stories);
6. Quality of contributions to knowledge databases;
7. Sharing and use of best practices;
8. Ease of employing quality staff;
9. General employee satisfaction (both user and support staff);
10. Tool availability;

11. Knowledge user complaints;
12. Knowledge user satisfaction;
13. Client satisfaction in quality of legal work;
14. Client satisfaction in supporting client-facing KM (portals, newsletters, seminars);
15. Perceived usefulness surveys – how KM tool helps users accomplish their objectives;
16. Effectiveness of sharing communities;
17. Perceived attitudes to failure; and
18. Perceived attitudes to knowledge hoarding or other barriers to knowledge sharing.

Annex 2

Ten Measure Design Tests[7]

1. The truth test – are we really measuring what we set out to measure?
2. The focus test – are we only measuring what we set out to measure?
3. The relevancy test – is it the right measure of the performance measure we want to track?
4. The consistency test – will the data always be collected in the same way whoever measures it?
5. The access test – is it easy to locate and capture the data needed to make the measurement?
6. The clarity test – is any ambiguity possible in interpreting the results?
7. The so-what test – can and will the data be acted upon?
8. The timeliness test – can the data be accessed rapidly and frequently enough for action?
9. The cost test – is the measure worth the cost of measurement?
10 The gaming test – is the measure likely to encourage undesirable or inappropriate behaviour?

Annex 3

Survey checklist

Design

- Plenty of open space and clear formatting
- Easy to read font
- Reasonable total length or divided into sections
- Start with easy questions

Questions

- Short and succinct
- Free of jargon
- Clear and specific
- More options than Yes/No (i.e. a five point Likert scale + 'don't know')

Avoid

- Double negatives
- Over-reliance on respondents' memories
- Leading questions
- Loaded questions
- Double-barrelled questions
- Splitting questions over two pages

Annex 4
Example and template

Business Goal	KM actions	Audience	Measure
Improve % of tenders won by 20% over next 5 financial years	Develop 'tenders' area of intranet, including knowledge pack, precedents/ standard clauses, after action learning wiki (within 10 weeks) Organise and support face-to-face AAR meetings following successful and unsuccessful tenders. Develop/improve thereafter (continuous)	Executive Board and Partnership Community of users	**Quantitative, leading (inputs)** Hits on 'tenders' intranet pages and dwell times (monthly) Downloads of precedents/ standard clauses (monthly) Numbers of contributions to the AAL wiki (monthly) Time spent by fee earners preparing tenders (using a specific time code) (monthly) Time spent by fee earners in developing 'tenders' package (using a specific time code) (monthly) (KM staff time is considered a sunk cost) **Quantitative, lagging (downstream/result)** Number of tenders won and percentage (monthly) **Qualitative, leading** Informal feedback discussions with user groups (monthly) User group feedback survey and meeting to measure satisfaction with quality and ease of use (annually) Post tender client feedback form (after each tender)

References

1. Kaplan, R. And Norton, D. (1992) The Balanced Scorecard – Measures That Drive Performance *Harvard Business Review January-February p71–79*
2. Kaplan, R. And Norton, D. (2001) Transforming the Balanced Scorecard from Performance Measurement to Strategic Management: Part 1 *Accounting Horizons* Vol 15 No 1 March 2001, p87–104
3. Kaplan, R. And Norton, D. (2001) Transforming the Balanced Scorecard from Performance Measurement to Strategic Management: Part 1 *Accounting Horizons* Vol 15 No 1 March 2001 p71
4. Rumizen, M. (2008) The Complete Idiot's Guide to Knowledge Management page 228

5. Although 'data' is strictly a plural term, I use the more common singular.
6. Note the difference in meaning of 'gaming' and 'gamification'. Gamification is the use of elements of game playing (psychology of engagement, competition, point scoring, badges, game levels) to drive behaviours in other fora, such as marketing, KM and other business systems. Gaming is

the, often subconscious, changes of behaviour when people aim to fulfil the measurement itself, rather than the objective behind the measurement.

7. Neely, A. et al (2002) *The Performance Prism. The Scorecard for Measuring and Managing Business Success* Financial Times, Prentice Hall, Harlow, via Chaffey, D. and Wood, S. (2005) *Business Information Management* Pearson Education Ltd p 529 via Russell, H. (2012) *Knowledge Management Handbook*, Law Society: London

Chapter 6:
Believing in organisational progress using data and anecdotes

By John Hovell, head of organisational development at BAE Systems

Since the 1990's, experts and organisations have been practising a multi-disciplinary field known as knowledge management. Many organisations ran KM experiments, progress was made, and the multi-disciplinary field began to grow. KM experts were often known as 'KMers', and they were quite excited about the potential of their growing discipline. Akin to most budding fields, many of the early experiments could be accomplished with little financial investment. As success grew, experts and organisations began discussions about KM investments.

From a perspective broader than KM, organisations often need to make difficult decisions about where to invest their money. This area of financial decision making is known as cost-benefit analysis. One standard approach for making cost-benefit decisions is the combination of return on investment (ROI) and break-even point. In this approach, executives and experts will compare many investment options by using numerous ratios and data points. As a result of this analysis and discussion, it is believed that wise financial decisions can be made about where to invest for maximum business benefit.

ROI, as a financial ratio, is simply calculated as 'Gain from Investment' minus 'Cost of Investment', which is then divided by 'Cost of Investment'. Break-even is the expected amount of time to pass before total revenue equals total costs. For example, if Option One will raise $1.2 million (evenly) over two years and will cost $1 million (evenly) over that time, then Option One has an ROI of 20 per cent and a break-even point of two years. If Option Two will raise $1.3 million (evenly) over two years and will cost $1 million (evenly) over that time, then Option Two has an ROI of 30 per cent and a break-even of two years. Most organisations will compare those numbers and invest in Option Two due to the greater return.

Often it is not that simple in reality. For example, what if Option One has noticeably more positive social impact than Option Two? A new ratio known as Social return on investment (SROI) was created for that reason. SROI includes 'narrative' or anecdotes and stories about the proposed investment. SROI involves stakeholders and decision makers in the process, effectively turning the decision making process into change management and a broader dialogue.

Social return on investment

As you might imagine, this approach brings more subjectivity into the decision making process. KM often creates intangible value, as opposed to measurable tangible value. Further, it can be a challenge to predict the stories and anecdotes that may result from KM initiatives. If knowledge flows well during a KM programme, you may find yourself trying to measure 'something that didn't happen'.

For example, a popular technology approach to knowledge management is Expertise Location Systems. One global defence organisation implemented a process and software approach to expertise location. The business case included the financial cost and potential business benefits. Most of the benefits centred on reduced time to make decisions and solve problems. Those benefits came true, which resulted in cost avoidance as opposed to cost savings. In other words, labour dollars were still spent, but productivity and efficiency increased due to the investment. Further, in this example, two expert engineers found each other through the system and solved a problem together. Then, growing their relationship, they collaborated to create a new business process which then resulted in winning new business and revenue growth for the organisation. Not only was it a positive story from a financial perspective, this particular new process also partnered with an external product and the combination was an overall service that resulted in lives being saved. It's hard to directly correlate and measure this success to the expertise location system, and yet it is quite likely that it would not have happened without it.

Expanding the ROI approach

There are other common approaches to measuring overall KM programmes. Two more examples are balanced scorecards and KM Maturity Models. The balanced scorecard approach again widens the ROI conversation to include overall financial, internal business, customer, and learning/growth objectives and measurements. KM Maturity Models are similar to other maturity models where there are five levels of maturity from which to assess your organisation. The levels increase in complexity from initiation to development to standardisation to optimisation to innovation. An organisation can review and assess its culture, process, and technology to determine how mature it is from a KM perspective. This is often accomplished through a process known as a knowledge audit. The intent is often to increase the organisation's level of KM maturity, which is then expected to produce increased ROI, to include the intangible or social perspectives. Both of these examples can be compared to the 'Triple Bottom Line'. The Triple Bottom Line is yet another financial perspective for measuring organisation success. This particular approach includes People, Profit, and Planet, to again expand upon the financial perspective.

Notice how all of the aforementioned approaches expand upon the single approach of ROI. In fact, all of the aforementioned approaches expand upon the perspective of financial analysis. Recent research helps us build upon these approaches. It has been found that the internal human system has as many neurotransmitters in the *enteric system* as in the spinal cord or peripheral nervous system.[1] In other words, the human 'gut' operates as a 'second brain' and both of these brains work together. It is helpful to relate these findings to the culture of making decisions in your organisation. For example, could you ask how much data has been necessary in the past for your organisation to make a financial investment decision? Are there examples of less data being available, where it was more of a 'gut feel' being used as rationalisation for experiments, investments, and decisions? Said even more directly, if the funding authorities and decision makers don't believe in a KM programme, or even a KM experiment, and the challenge is to proactively prove ROI, then it is quite likely that the funding will go elsewhere.

One of the most common KM approaches is known as Communities of Practice (CoP). A CoP is a voluntary group of people that become a community to practise a shared topic or interest. A large automotive business invested in a global CoP programme. This investment was made at little cost in an effort to try and reduce the cost of the business. The communities built trust and connected with each other for years, although produced little financial cost savings. Until one year when a business challenge was shared across two CoPs. The two CoPs took the challenge and creatively designed a new way to ship four times more car frames in a single locomotive compared to current shipping practices. This innovation saved the organisation millions of dollars, especially as it was shared across all of the countries in which it operated. The 'allowance' for these CoPs to exist set a cultural tone for groups to work together and it was that belief that resulted in the cost savings, as opposed to funding a single initiative to determine the cost savings approach.

These examples provide evidence that ROI is a helpful and yet limited view of an organisational environment. Employee engagement and customer delight can be quite difficult to predict, quantify, and measure. And yet, quantitative examples exist such as time savings, speed to competency, increased networking, increased output, increased quality, increased sales, and decreased costs. Michael Zack's research at Northeastern University probably stated it best to say that KM has a direct impact on Operational Efficiency and Operational Efficiency has a direct impact on Financial Performance, so it's a two-step measurement. For the time savings perspective, McKinsey research measured the average time employees spend checking email, communicating, searching for information/knowledge, collaborating with others and completing role-specific tasks. Their results found 20–25 per cent of that time is wasted and could be improved through KM approaches. That 20–25 per cent operational efficiency improvement would have a direct impact on financial performance for any organisation.

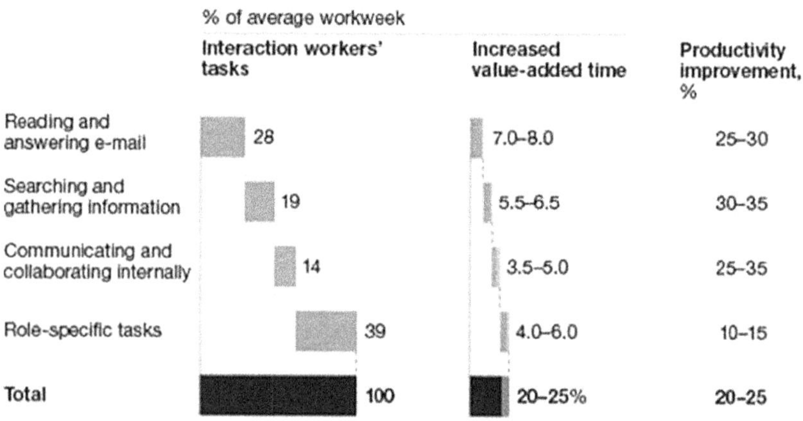

Source: International Data Corporation (IDC); McKinsey Global Institute analysis

Given these examples, although it may be ideal to have a formal, organisation-wide KM programme, it is often that case that KM approaches are best applied to specific organisational challenges. For example, one global conglomerate found that 49 per cent of its employee population was going to retire in the next five to eight years. This organisation feared a catastrophic loss of knowledge and capability, so it implemented a global knowledge sharing process. They partnered with other organisations to find a world-class four-step knowledge retention process. It is a team based approach, so after successfully completing several dozen teams, the internal facilitators partnered with the internal finance department to research and validate any cost savings. The partnership was able to prove and document a $121,000 cost avoidance per knowledge transfer team.

Measurement experts will often talk about indicators and innovative ways of gathering data. The primary categories of indicators are leading, lagging, in-process, and output/outcome. As opposed to expanding the conversation from financial to non-financial, these indicators attempt to broaden the conversation from only 'looking forward in time' to past, present, and future data points. Leading indicators such as the percentage of employee attrition and the number of innovations can help to predict the future environment. Lagging indicators such as hours of time saved and the percentage of reduction in audit findings can help to show progress over time. In-process indicators such as the number of active knowledge transfer teams can help explain the current state. Output and outcome measures such as the number of new contracts and the number of process improvements can again expand from quantitative measures to more qualitative, narrative type measures.

Leading

- Turnover Percent
- Number of Actions (from Knowledge Transfer, Learn from Experience)
- Number of Innovations

Lagging

- Percentage of Reduction in Audit Findings
- Amount of time saved
- Percentage of Increase in Great Workplace Results

In-Process

- Number of Knowledge Transfer Teams
- Number of Learn from Experience Events

Output / Outcome

- Number of Programs Won
- Documented quality improvements
- Cumulative cost reduction

Conclusion

In conclusion, Stan Garfield's KM ROI article[2] is the quintessential read for KM ROI discussion. It is a long term collection of articles and conversations that has been maintained for decades. Overall, KM ROI is a challenging conversation and often an overly limited perspective for making KM decisions. Qualitative, quantitative, tangible, and intangible factors must be considered, which are often difficult to predict and measure. If funding authorities, decision makers and the organisation don't 'believe' (e.g. enteric system in addition to the brain) and the conversation is focused on ROI, then it may be a long and challenging road ahead. Anecdotes about specific organisational wins are often the most effective approach, especially if they tell a story of improvements in productivity, cost, quality, and/or speed. For most organisations, the KM ROI perspective can be simply stated as 'it will be more expensive in the long run if we do NOT invest in these KM approaches'. Knowledge is the lifeblood of any organisation, leaving the flow of that knowledge up to chance is not helpful for the organisation. The unfortunate narrative of knowledge inefficiency is likely to be an emotion (as well as financial cost) paid by its employees and customers. The positive perspective is that optimal knowledge flow can be documented, measured, and felt by employees, organisations, and customers.

References

1. Hashazy, A., "Think Twice: How the Gut's 'Second Brain' Influences Mood and Well-Being" Feb. 2010. See: https://www.scientificamerican.com/article/gut-second-brain/
2. Garfield, S., "KM's not dead, but talking about its ROI should be" Nov. 2015. See: https://www.linkedin.com/pulse/kms-dead-talking-its-roi-should-stan-garfield

Chapter 7:
The case against ROI for knowledge management

By Stan Garfield, knowledge management author, speaker, and community leader

The subject of how to compute the return on investment for knowledge management has been around since the start of the field. My view is that it is important to define and communicate the benefits of a KM program, and measure and report on progress, but that proving ROI should not be the point.

It's possible to compute the ROI of a narrowly-defined project requiring capital investment, such as building a new plant or buying a new piece of equipment. But for broader programs which integrate people, process, and technology components, and work with other broad programs such as learning, talent development, and finance to improve the effectiveness of the organisation, ROI is ill-suited.

'What will be the ROI of your KM program?' is the wrong question. Better questions include:

- Why should we implement a KM program?
- What are the benefits?
- How will it help our organisation accomplish its key objectives?
- How will our organisation improve as a result?
- How will our people's needs, opportunities, and challenges be met?

Do we ask what the ROI is for the human resources or finance departments? What about the ROI for the email or phone systems?

For example, if we were to eliminate the HR department because its ROI is too low, what might happen? From 'The 5 most dangerous legal mistakes HR makes' by *Business Management Daily*, here are three potential problems which could arise by leaving personnel administration to the individual managers:

- Wrongly classifying certain employees as exempt from the Fair Labor Standards Act and, thus, ineligible for overtime pay;
- I-9 form mistakes; and
- Messy firings – the biggest cause of employee lawsuits.

Having trained professionals in the HR department can help avoid these and many other costly errors. But computing the ROI on preventing lawsuits is not possible.

The right focus

So, what should we do instead of focusing on ROI?

1. Make a logical case for how the initiative will help achieve the key business objectives of the organisation. For example, if the top three objectives are increasing profits, accelerating sales, and improving customer satisfaction, explain how the elements of the program will have a positive impact on these. If profits increase, sales accelerate, and customer satisfaction improves, and there is a rational explanation for how knowledge management supported these results, then take partial credit. On the other hand, if the business results are not achieved, then the fact that KM did well will not likely be well-received. You can try to argue that things would have been even worse without KM, but that would be a hollow victory.
2. Establish a plausible scenario and then extrapolate the benefits. For example:
    - If we save one project from repeating the same mistakes as previous projects, that could save $2 million, which will more than pay for the program. If we repeat this, the impact on profits is very large.
    - If by responding quickly to an opportunity with a proven solution using acknowledged experts, we win one $10 million project that we otherwise would have lost, that's incremental revenue of $10 million. If we repeat this, the impact on revenue is very large.
    - If by ensuring that the best engineering product knowledge is reused, we avoid one product recall, we save the company hundreds of millions of dollars.

    This type of business case can be very persuasive. Note, though, that it is not a strict ROI analysis. You can't prove that the sole cause of any outcome was KM, and you can't prove that a costly recall was avoided if it never happened. But you can point out that the probabilities of positive outcomes are significantly increased through KM.

3. Choose the most relevant benefits from the list below and ask the program sponsor to confirm that these are the right ones. Tailor your efforts to achieve these desired benefits:
    - Enabling better and faster decision making;
    - Making it easy to find relevant information and resources;
    - Reusing ideas, documents, and expertise;
    - Avoiding redundant effort;
    - Avoiding making the same mistakes twice;
    - Taking advantage of existing experience;
    - Communicating important information widely and quickly;
    - Promoting standard, repeatable processes, and procedures;
    - Providing methods, tools, templates, techniques, and examples;
    - Making scarce expertise widely available;
    - Showing customers how knowledge is used for their benefit;
    - Accelerating delivery to customers;
    - Enabling the organisation to leverage its size;
    - Making the organisation's best problem-solving experiences reusable; and
    - Stimulating innovation and growth.
4. Define the most painful problems that knowledge management can help prevent, such as:
    - Product recalls;
    - Injuries or deaths;
    - Lawsuits;
    - Unprofitable products and services;
    - Low employee morale;
    - Lost customers;
    - Damage to the brand;
    - Inability to attract or retain talent;

- Diminished productivity, revenue, growth, profit margin, shareholder valued; and
- Becoming a takeover target.

5. Before launching a program, tell stories that show the value it will provide. After the program starts, tell stories of early success. As the program matures, document wins using the voices of actual users.
6. Define relevant metrics for all stated objectives, and report regularly on performance against those metrics. Pair operational metrics with business impact metrics and correlate good performance in the KM program with good results for the business. Measure the benefits of your KM efforts.
7. Make a sound business case. For example:
   - Do we want our people to be able to readily find deliverables from previous projects so that they can reuse them, and people who can provide useful advice on how to deliver the next one?
   - Do we want anyone who has a question, seeks a resource, or requires help to be able to easily, quickly, and reliably get what they need?
   - Do we want to avoid redundant effort, repeating the same mistakes over and over, and keeping important information from reaching the very people who need it?
8. Work with analytics experts, statisticians, and academicians to produce correlations between desired knowledge-sharing actions and desired results, including employee advancement, project success, and financial results. For example, Kai Riemer of the University of Sydney has a forthcoming paper which states 'a range of empirical studies in organisations have shown that this type of social capital is associated with better individual performance evaluations, greater promotion chances and higher compensation payments as well as an increased team performance'.
9. Do a one-time study to show the business benefits. Caterpillar commissioned a one-time study by an independent consulting firm to identify the benefits and ROI for two established communities of practice: Joints and Fasteners and Dealer Service Training. The results were:
   - Qualitative ROI: Productivity (up 40 per cent), Cost (reduced 25 per cent), Speed (up 15 per cent), Quality (up 4 per cent).

  - Tangible ROI: 200 per cent for internal CoPs; 700 per cent for external CoPs.

  Based on these results, the Caterpillar KM program was justified. There is no need for ongoing collection and reporting of ROI, since it has been done once.

10. Read and consider applying the ideas expressed in the following articles, posts, and books.

Literature review

1. My former HP colleague, Andrew Gent, wrote *ROI: the Sad Case for KM*. Andrew's words are just as relevant now as when he wrote them in back in 2007.

> More and more frequently I hear calls for proof of the 'ROI' (Return on Investment) of knowledge management. I hear it within my own company; I hear it from KM practitioners in other companies; I even hear KM consultants espousing the importance and benefits of calculating ROI to demonstrate knowledge management's contribution to the business bottom line. This concerns me. Not because I don't believe KM has value -- it obviously does! -- but because ROI is a specific type of business measurement that overemphasizes the direct-to-bottom-line component of KM while completely ignoring (and discrediting) the rest. KM certainly contributes indirectly to the bottom line, as it contributes to many other aspects of the company's fiscal and intellectual diversity and health. But that is not its primary goal. This call for ROI is part of a larger tendency within corporations today to 'align' KM with business operations. By that I mean making KM a tool used by business management to ensure the optimal and efficient exercise of business processes.
>
> Now, I have no objections to KM supporting business processes. Clearly, that is the primary use of knowledge and the company wants to encourage anything that contributes to the bottom line. But that is not all that KM is about. KM also significantly contributes to the breadth of knowledge, experience, and expertise of its employees. It contributes to the resilience and responsiveness of the company to changes in the business environment by strengthening its core intellectual capabilities. It impacts business processes both direct and indirect. And it establishes a culture and channels for distributing business intelligence at lightning speed. The problem is the measuring. Managers don't measure things for intellectual stimulation. They measure them so they can make changes and confirm the results. Managers also tend to think high-level. If ROI is what you are measuring, then that is the goal (not a goal, the goal). That is not a slam against managers, it is just an attribute of their job: to think clearly and succinctly and not get bogged down in details.

The results, if you are not careful, can be both dramatic and unfortunate. The analogy that comes to mind is college. If you see the goal of college being to get a job (your ROI), then there really is no need for English, history, languages, or even science -- depending upon your target profession. However, if you see the goal of college as expanding your knowledge and broadening your character, not only will it have a strong indirect impact on your employability, but your opportunities will be far more flexible and adaptive to the business environment when you graduate. Business opportunities fluctuate on a cyclic basis. At one point, there was a strong need for engineers. But if you went to school specifically for that career, the market was pretty much saturated 4-5 years later when you graduated. Ditto MBAs and other focused degrees. I pity the poor Cobol programmer trying to break into the web era. Or Algol, PL/1, Pascal... So just as the goal of college is to teach capabilities, not specific skills; the goal of KM is to facilitate knowledge development and transfer, not solely to apply knowledge to the product pipeline.

The success or 'return' of a KM program is the cumulative benefits -- both short and long-term on the company and its employees. This is a very hard concept for line-of-business managers to grasp. They understand it when they feel its absence -- the recent rebirth of KM within American companies runs a parallel course to the enthusiasm for the business fads of downsizing, rightsizing, and outsourcing in the late 80's and 90's. Many companies followed the trend only to find that the intelligence of the corporation had left with its employees. The need for knowledge management became apparent. I believe it is the responsibility of KM professionals to avoid the rush to ROI and make sure both the direct and indirect 'returns' of KM are recognized and re-established as objectives.

2 *Selling KM: Lessons from Experience* from Richard Cross

Never trust someone who says 'Show me the ROI' or 'You can only measure what you manage' Anthropologists maintain that in every culture there are apparently rational questions that mask hostile intent. 'Show me the ROI' or 'Yes, but how do you measure it?' generally fall into this category. When confronted with these types, start to get alarmed. The most important point I recall from my sales training is that a customer's concern in a complex sale is risk. According to my sales training mentor, Roger Sugden, consequences (risks of going ahead with you) must be managed. Most lurk behind the surface. Roger also emphasized that difficulty stating, quibbling over minor points (like the pantone color of a slide), asking for demonstrable ROI, and jargon bashing (we offered TQM training at that time) could also be early warnings on risk, customer insecurity, and lack of their (or your) credibility.

Price concerns and guaranteed ROI then become respectable and convenient ways to express concerns over consequences. It's easier for people to tell you that they have decided not to buy because of these issues than to explain issues such as mistrust, scars from mistakes made before, politics, hassle, not interested, risk to career or company, or the simple fact that *they don't like you*. Consequences are psychological issues in a person's mind. They are not in the real world - only the customer can resolve them. In selling KM and TQM, Roger would advise me to *help the customer, not resolve the problem on his behalf.* He would also say to get the real concerns out in the open, and look to develop trust rather than engage in futile intellectualizing about ROI.

In an AOK dialogue hosted by Jerry Ash, Hubert Saint-Onge concluded that 'I fully subscribe to the need to measure all that can be measured but I don't believe that you can only manage what you can measure. As a matter of fact, I find this one of the most mindless dictums to ever be uttered by people who appear to be otherwise reasonably coherent.' My bottom line: *the purpose is to improve, not prove.*

3. *What's Your Return on Knowledge?* by Don Cohen

Leaders of the knowledge-based organisations that have the most vibrant KM programs approach the measurement problem by accepting soft indicators that knowledge management is earning its keep rather than demanding hard numbers that may be misleading. They do insist that the programs be evaluated, but they accept anecdotes about successful (or failed) knowledge reuse, stories of productive (or unproductive) collaborative projects, and surveys of employee and customer satisfaction as the best indicators of value. They realize that a telling anecdote is a better 'measure' than a precise but irrelevant number. Knowing what you're striving for with your knowledge management makes it much easier to determine whether you're getting value for the money spent—even if the ROI never shows up on a balance sheet.

4. *Rethinking ROI: The Metrics of Intangible Assets* by Art Murray

Next to 'What is the meaning of life?' perhaps the toughest question we KMers get asked is 'What's the ROI (return on investment) for all this KM stuff?' At the project level, it's rather straightforward. You can measure what goes in and what comes out (efficiency and effectiveness). You can compare the results before your KM pilot initiative and after, and take it from there. Justifying KM to promote fast learning and innovation enterprise-wide is another matter entirely.

5. *Why measure the value of KM?* by Chris Collison

I can remember the second year of BP's KM program some years ago, when we were asked to demonstrate $100m of business value through the application of KM approaches and tools. We did this by asking senior managers, directors and VPs who had been applying KM tools (mostly with some support from our team) for anecdotes and stories with $ value attached. Many of them did and when we passed the $250m barrier we stopped counting. Was it scientific? No. Did it comply with Generally Accepted Accounting Principles? No. Did they have credibility as stories? Absolutely yes – because of who was telling them. Did the stories inspire others and give momentum to what was going on? Definitely. However, one senior VP in Mergers and Acquisitions refused to be drawn on the specific contribution that KM had made to a recent acquisition. 'It's a big number' he said, 'but it's in there with the spaghetti...' (meaning, the other approaches that had also been brought to bear on this acquisition). I have a lot of sympathy with that view. Whilst I recognize that we need to be able to illustrate the value that knowledge sharing brings, with compelling examples and stories, my preference would be to commit the minimum time necessary to the activity of measurement. Like that manager – I'd rather than get on with eating the spaghetti than don a white coat and spectrophotometrically analyze the Bolognese sauce.

6. *Knowledge Management – Measuring Return on Investment* by Steve Dale

Of course, the problem remains that not all changes can be measured in strictly cash value terms, which is what many people consider to be the true meaning of ROI. I go back to the point I made earlier – how do you measure the value of a conversation or some information shared? The answer is, you don't, and the sooner that everyone recognises this the better. Measuring impact can be just as important as measuring value. The impact might be things like improved customer satisfaction (measured using surveys), or less time to complete a task, or improved staff morale (measured using surveys). Any of these can – and potentially will – have an effect in terms of cash value to the organisation, but I firmly believe that converting impact to cash value is an exercise in futility, since more often than not, the formulae and algorithms have too many variables. So, in terms of 'ROI', think 'Return on Impact' rather than Return on Investment when considering Knowledge management strategies, and develop the strategy from the starting point of getting staff to justify the present status quo.

7. *Managing by Numbers: ROI and the death of business* by Patrick Lambe

So when we put up our e-business investment proposals, our e-learning proposals, and our knowledge management proposals, the CEO wants to see an ROI analysis, and the CFO will be doing a surreptitious EVA. All very objective, terribly easy to decide. The trouble is, when you look at them very closely, very few aspects of real-world enterprise actually run on numbers, and ROIs tell you surprisingly little about whether you really should invest – especially once you move outside the ambit of simply buying something. The passion for ROIs, which is often justified in the service of a simple purchase that has attributable profits, becomes positively dangerous when it is used in the service of complex investments, business innovation, capability development, or infrastructure investment – as it happens, all characteristics of e-business, e-learning and knowledge management initiatives.

8. *Rethinking ROI: Managing Risk and Rewards in KM Initiatives* by John I. Alber

As you can see, changing the calculus can yield widely different results. That is troubling enough in itself. There is plenty of room to bamboozle a technology committee or a management group, just in the math alone. But there is a more fundamental problem with any ROI calculation: while the upfront costs are easy to determine, the net benefits are, essentially, an exercise in creating fiction. The more intangible the benefits involved, the more likely they are to be wrong.

9. *Why You Should Stop Using ROI* by Bennett Stewart

I come not to praise ROI. I come to bury it, for a simple reason. A company that aims to maximize its ROI will always tend to underinvest, under-innovate, under-scale, and under-grow, and leave value on the table. It may even become vulnerable to a hostile takeover or a toppling by upstart rivals. ROI is like shooting percentage in basketball. To maximize it, you'd just take a sure layup and stop shooting. You can't improve on 100 per cent. You'd pass the ball even when you have a better shot than any other player. Managers judged by ROI will act the same. They'll stop short of taking all the shots they should. Business units already earning high returns will tend to pass by growth they ought to pursue. The bottom line is, all companies should aim to maximize their EVA profit – even when that comes at the expense of ROI, as it almost always does.

10. *Methods for Measuring Intangible Assets* by Karl-Erik Sveiby

> The main problem with measurement systems is that it is not possible to measure social phenomena with anything close to scientific accuracy. All measurement systems, including traditional accounting, have to rely on proxies, such as dollars, euros, and indicators that are far removed from the actual event or action that caused the phenomenon. This creates a basic inconsistency between managers' expectations, the promises made by the method developers and what the systems can actually achieve and makes all these systems very fragile and open to manipulation. Therefore, the first question for any one embarking on a measurement initiative must be: What is the purpose of our measuring initiative?

Chapter 8: Winning the war by avoiding the battles – Focusing on the I in ROI

By Andrew Gent, lead information architect at VoltDB

Let's be realistic: the main goal of measuring ROI is to justify the costs of a program or initiative. Before the fact, ROI measured as a projection of expected returns is used to justify an initial investment. Whereas after the fact, ROI measured as actual returns is often used to validate continued investment, under the assumption that the return/investment ratio will continue to follow a positive trend.

However, as pointed out earlier in this book, measuring the indirect results of knowledge management initiatives is a tenuous business at best. And even if you establish a model for comparing cost and manpower against outcome, there are still two hurdles you are likely to face. First, management types who require ROI evaluations tend to think in hard numbers – cash – and are skeptical (or outright resistant) to 'creative' accounting methods. Second, unlike other types of projects, such as hardware or infrastructure, KM initiatives are not a one-time investment. They are ongoing efforts requiring nurture and care. Even if you manage to justify an initial investment, you are often required to return, year after year, to compete with other line-of-business proposals in the face of the seemingly capricious budget knife.

One way to avoid this cyclic battle is, rather than focusing on the return on the investment, to focus on the investment itself. That is, make the activities resilient and self-sufficient so they are less susceptible to the vagaries of budget exercises.

Eliminating the need for investment entirely is not possible. But achieving greater sustainability is, by using the same methods advocated by other 'green' movements: recycle, reuse, and employ renewable resources. In other words, rather than seeing KM projects as separate and requiring dedicated resources, find ways to reuse and enhance existing people and processes to encourage knowledge sharing.

What follows are four examples of approaches that can harden KM projects and reduce their dependence on the ever elusive corporate dollar, pound, euro, or yuan. Those approaches are:

- Embedded KM;
- Design to zero;
- Reuse what exists; and
- DIY KM.

Embedded KM

The most obvious approach to sustainability is *embedded KM*, where you embed knowledge management practices into the existing business processes. The key benefits from embedded KM are:

- Rapid adoption; and
- Tied to business metrics.

An added advantage is that – if done properly – there is little or no need for training since there is little or no change to behaviour. If you embed the knowledge management procedures in the existing operational processes, knowledge sharing becomes an integral part of employees' day-to-day work.

Let's look at an example. Say your business process already includes reviews at key milestones. It is likely that certain documents are required for the review: project overview, costs, schedule, etc. There may already be a template for these documents. If one of your KM goals is to make employees more aware of other projects to increase sharing knowledge and reducing overlap, one easy way to do this is simply collect the project overviews from each review to create a project catalog.

On the positive side, since the documents are already being created and the review is an existing milestone in the process, the only work needed to implement the project catalog is creating the repository (a one-time event) and influencing the review managers to post the appropriate documents in it. Working with the managers responsible for the reviews, it should be only a slight modification to the standard process to implement.

However, collecting information is only part of the solution. To have any impact at all, the information has to be *used*. And, quite frankly, a directory full of unsorted documents is neither particularly useful nor appealing to anyone. So to complete the circle there are at least two additional steps:

- Add steps to the project lifecycle to remind team members to use the repository. (Again, this is best done by tweaking existing process steps or milestones, such as requirements gathering, design, and/or implementation stages); and
- Make the repository easy to use.

The latter step sounds deceptively simple, but is really the crux of the issue. For the repository to be useful, it needs to be searchable and sortable in some meaningful way. The way to do this is to provide metadata about the documents; classifications such as *industry*, *country*, *client name*, etc.

Rarely is the interesting information clearly or consistently labeled in business documents. So the only way to effectively add the metadata is to:

- Require users to fill out the metadata for each item; and
- Modify the templates used to include specific fields for the metadata (and get the authors to use them correctly).

As you can see, a simple update to an existing process can suddenly become quite complex. The more fields you add, the less likely people are to cooperate by filling them in. Getting people to fill out input forms including metadata is extremely hard; they are either put off by the form or they fill out the form with incomplete or misleading information. The same problem occurs when templates contain embedded fields. Making sure everyone uses the new templates and uses them correctly is a significant training and communication task. The more fields are added the more monitoring is required to make sure the submissions are complete and meaningful.

So a simple 'improvement' to the system can quickly burgeon into extended activities to maintain and support the process. Conceptually, you can view a 'capture and reuse' program such as described as being positioned somewhere on a curve from *no modification* to *optimised for reuse*.

When there is little or no modification to the content, very little management needs to be applied and the process is highly sustainable. Unfortunately, this also leaves the work of providing relevance up to the users of the content, which is often too much to make the effort worthwhile. (In other words, the system may go unused and have little value.)

To make the information usable, it needs to be modified to provide relevance. However, doing this requires changes to the process by which it is captured, adding new challenges in communicating the new process, training the users, and encouraging submissions. The content becomes more usable, but significant, ongoing effort is required to enforce and monitor the submissions, since the effort is now put on the contributors rather than the end users. In other words, an unsustainable process.

The trick is to find the middle ground (indicated by the shaded box in the following diagram), where the content is usable *enough* and the contribution process simple *enough* that people can and will manage their own use of the system. Experience teaches us that this 'sweet spot' can be an extremely narrow segment of the curve and very hard to hit.

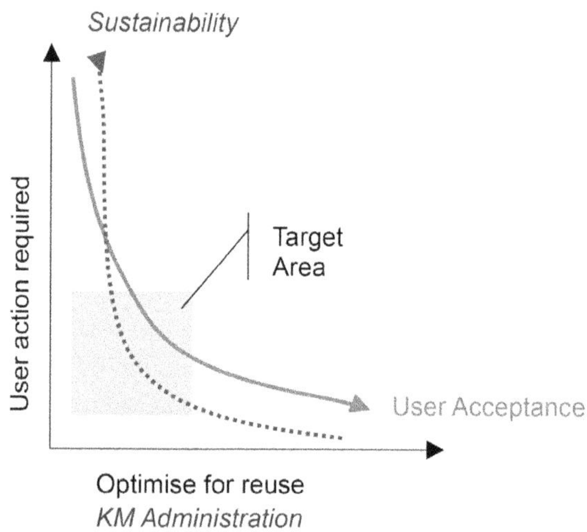

As this example demonstrates, processes to manage explicit knowledge, although they sound simple, can quickly evolve into complex, unsustainable programs from only minor 'improvements'. So let's consider an alternative.

Rather than trying to make all project knowledge available to anyone, what if you simply try to expand the current knowledge base incrementally over time? Rather than collecting the review documents, why not include at least one reviewer from an unrelated project to each review? This might be an architect, implementer, or project manager – as long as that person can provide an objective, outside view of the project progress.

The consequence is that the outside reviewer takes this knowledge back to their own project where it may or may not be used immediately. But it sticks with that person for a long time, due to the direct and active interaction they have with the other team.

What is required to make this program work? Initiating the program can be difficult because it requires diplomacy. On the other hand, it involves only a limited number of people; primarily, a sponsor to convince management of the efficacy of including outside reviewers. But once you modify the review process, the program becomes essentially self-managing from a KM perspective. The project management teams are responsible for ensuring outside reviewers are included and with each review, little by little, knowledge is shared across the organisation.

Design to zero

Another approach to sustainable KM projects is 'design to zero'. It is impossible to start a business initiative with *no* resources. Even if it is only your own time and attention as a KM manager, there is some expenditure required.

Every new project requires a 'bump' to get it started. This includes training, hardware and software expenditures, project management, etc. The problem is that budget planning often only accounts for the short term (two, three, or perhaps five years at most). For projects with a defined endpoint, this is alright. However, KM projects are intended to run indefinitely. (It doesn't make sense to stop sharing knowledge after three years, does it?)

This means that, although it may not show up on the plan of record, the KM program must account for the ongoing maintenance of long-term projects. If you load up your KM program with management of ongoing initiatives, there are two negative consequences:

- When budgets and headcount are cut, you have no choice but to abandon one or more of the initiatives, usually bringing the program to a screeching halt. Without the expected leadership and constant 'push', non-sustainable programs fail when the budget stops; and
- Even if budgets stay the same, after a while you have no spare resources to start new programs. Even when a good idea comes along your KM team is fully booked and you do not have sufficient resources to start anything new without impacting maintenance of existing programs.

How do you avoid this dilemma? The key is to design each project – from the beginning – to reach zero cost. That doesn't mean management goes to zero or that residual effort goes to zero, but that the program is designed to become self-supporting at a set point in time.

Rather than planning for the first year 'bump' and letting maintenance trail on indefinitely, plan from the beginning that management of the program and responsibility for its ongoing success is transferred to the appropriate people within the organisation. Sometimes this means the project may need a bigger expense up front (as shown in the graph below). But the benefit is that the project then becomes self-sustaining and the KM team can move on to tackle other tasks.

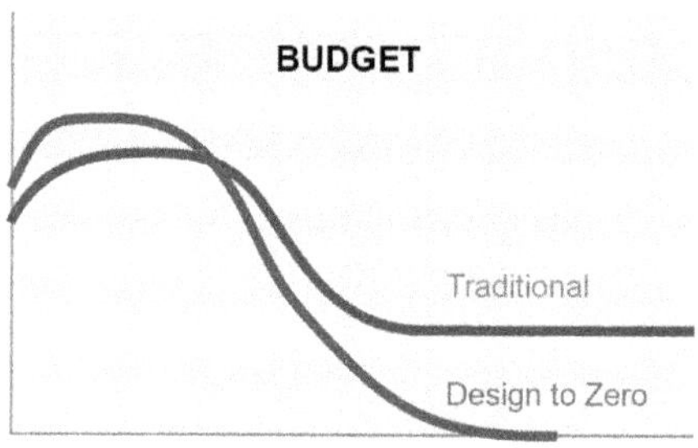

Going back to our example of embedded KM, it is not sufficient to have the idea to invite architects from other disciplines to the project reviews. You need to make sure that the organisation running the reviews understands that their success depends on this outside participation and, therefore, they are responsible for making sure it continues once the program is off the ground.

As with any sustainable practice, not all projects are suited for design to zero. But far more projects are candidates than one might expect. The trick is to look for the part of the organisation (usually lines of business) that will benefit most from the effort. Engage them early in the planning, so they feel responsible for its success. Then get them to commit to ongoing management as part of their regular business cycle.

Reuse what exists

The next principle for sustainable projects is to reuse what already exists. This is similar to embedded KM. But rather than applying KM to other business processes, reuse looks for existing knowledge and knowledge sharing within the business and works to enhance and strengthen them.

At its simplest, reuse can be finding existing repositories of knowledge (such as sales databases, or project reviews) and making them more widely available to others within the organisation who need the information. For large corporations, simply knowing what customers the company is engaged with can be helpful to others.

Mind you, loosening individual organisations' grips on such information is often the single most challenging obstacle to such efforts. Part of the initial 'bump' for such an effort is identifying the pertinent information from such systems. For example, in sales databases, the revenue numbers are too sensitive for wide distribution, even internally. However, the names and descriptions of the companies and what products they are using is both less sensitive and more widely applicable to other internal corporate groups.

Another, less obvious, example of reusable assets is existing formal and informal interactions between employees. Corporate events, group meetings, and retreats – although unrelated to KM per se – are fertile ground for informal knowledge sharing. No matter what the primary goal of the meeting might be, adding a KM 'track' to the agenda provides an opportunity to reinforce existing KM initiatives as well promote new ones for practically free.

Another use of existing face-to-face meetings is to encourage knowledge sharing among practitioners. Even if you can't get on the agenda, consider sponsoring a knowledge sharing breakfast, lunch, or coffee break for your key audience.[1] These can be informal social gatherings where practitioners simply get to know each other and swap tales of work in the trenches. Or you can provide some structure to encourage sharing. For example, ask for volunteers to give five minute 'war stories' about one significant episode in their work experience. You can even offer a prize for the best story to further fuel the conversation. Compared to the cost of organising, scheduling, and funding a separate 'knowledge management face-to-face', a prize or two at an existing get-together is an insignificant investment.

DIY KM

Finally, what do you do if there is *no* investment? When no separate KM practice exists, how do businesses solve the knowledge management problem?

These questions are most pertinent to smaller companies: startups, consultancies, etc. Larger companies that do not have a centralised KM function will often delegate the responsibility to the individual line organisations. But even there, the individual businesses usually have sufficient critical mass to support concentrated, if separate, KM initiatives.

For smaller companies, there is simply not enough cycles available to maintain a separate effort. That doesn't mean knowledge sharing is not necessary. It just means it needs to be done on a 'best effort' basis. In these cases it pays to adopt a do-it-yourself approach.

The advantage of smaller companies is that everyone tends to feel a commitment to the enterprise as a whole, not just their particular role. Everyone has ideas and innovative solutions can surface quickly. On the downside, everyone has an opinion and it may be hard to get consensus for efforts, such as knowledge sharing, that have no clear responsible individual.

Take advantage of the energy and enthusiasm of the participants. Wikis and other free (or close to free) unstructured social network tools such as Slack may not be appropriate for larger organisations – they require more setup, structure, and guidelines to keep the information structured with hundreds or thousands of users. But they can be ideal for small groups. If they get disorganised it is easy to restructure or set up guidelines on the fly when working with 20-30 people (something that is not possible with 400, 500, or more).

And don't be upset if tools get tried and abandoned. Again, use the enthusiasm of the users to overcome whatever downside and effort is required to switch to something better. The key is not to attempt to apply too much structure or limitations on the system early on. Let the users get started and become dependent on the benefits of the process. If necessary, you can adapt and refine the process later. Again, what works for small groups does *not* necessarily work for larger organisations. Understanding the capabilities (and constraints) of your audience is important when selecting an appropriate strategy.

Summary

Evaluating the relative success or failure of individual projects is critical. It can help validate that your resources are being applied correctly and show where to make appropriate adjustments. However, ROI as a method for measuring knowledge management programs against other corporate initiatives is a perilous enterprise.

But it is useful to note that the preceding techniques are not *just* beneficial for avoiding budget battles. In fact, they reinforce fundamental principles of successful KM programs in general. Sustainable KM practices help avoid creating extra work, integrate knowledge sharing practices into the core workflow of your target audience, and balance KM ideals with the practical limits of people's attention span. Frequently, the pragmatic choice of a 'good enough' solution produces faster and better results than a 'correct' solution that requires extensive promotion, training, and process change to implement.

References

1. A vivid demonstration of the power of such informal gatherings can be found in Brown and Duguid's *The Social Life of Information* (Harvard Business Review Press, Boston, 2000), where they discuss the example of Xerox field reps meeting socially off-hours to share the experiences, issues, and solutions learned from repairing copiers.

Chapter 9:

An ecological approach to understanding impact in knowledge management practice

By Professor Snowden, director of the Cynefin Centre at Bangor University and chief scientific officer at Cognitive Edge

Measurement is a complex issue at the best of times, but in the field of knowledge management especially so. There is a question is to what can be measured and how, but there is also the matter of the impact of those measures. Strathern's variation on Goodhart's Law states: 'Any measure which becomes a target ceases to be a measure.' A large body of research states that when people are working for explicit goals it destroys intrinsic motivation. The article will identify a key differences between outcome, output, and vector measures. Then on top of what we measure we have the question of what is invested. Not just the conventional difference between actual and opportunity costs but also the wider gambit of types of knowledge and the longer term consequences for the organisation. Using complexity science as a basis this article will look at some of the radical new approaches emerging from our growing understanding of systems which are inherently uncertain.

When I finally got myself together to write this article I had just delivered a keynote on the role of knowledge management to a chapter of the Project Management Association in Milan, Italy. I opened the presentation with a renaissance painting of Daniel in the lion's den and confessed to the audience that I had long used their PMBOK (Project Management Body of Knowledge) approach as a near perfect example of how not to do it; many agreed with me! The week before I had been a keynote speaker at the largest, and longest running, KM conference in the world in Washington DC in the immediate aftermath of the post-fact, post-rational, post-human election of Trump to the leadership of the free world. It was the 20th year of the event and the 20th year in which I had been a keynote. I told my Milanese project managers of this and pointed out that during those decades I had seen multiple cycles of knowledge management initiatives – all of which had failed over varying time intervals. The knowledge teams, laid off during conditions of scarcity, form consultancy groups to sell what they claim to have achieved before their relevance to the business was brought into question. But the need to manage knowledge in a changing world, with high staff turnover and a challenging business environment, is persistent and a new knowledge team will be formed. Like their predecessors they would focus on the codification of knowledge, the creation of communities of practice and so on. The cycle then repeats and the new team attempt to justify their programmes by seeking to create a direct connection between their programme and financial returns. So to be clear this is a contrarian article, a challenge to the idea of measurement, and a proposal to take a different, more natural approach. But it isn't idealistic, it argues to imbed knowledge management in the *way we do things around here* so that its role is accepted in the same way as these days we assume employees need access to computers; knowledge needs to become a hygiene factor, not a luxury.

Now the conventional approach is understandable, the norms of ROI measurement are established business practice for most overhead functions within organisations. They are under more pressure than operational budgets. Charged with setting up a knowledge programme it is understandable, even excusable, to copy what other people *say* they have done at conferences, in books, in the popular literature. Few if any have bothered to validate the retrospective claims for knowledge management officers. I suspect they all know, or are at least informed by the infamous Nonaka SECI (or BA) model that talks about the knowledge creation cycle. In this which tacit knowledge is assumed to be able to be made explicit and thus more readily distributed and accessed. I am certain few, if any, check into insights from cognitive science or anthropology which are more relevant than cases defined by those with an interest in claiming success. In my opinion neither Nonaka or his various followers really took on board a key statement from the modern originator of the tacit-explicit distinction. Writing in *Knowing and Being* Polanyi clearly stated:

> *While tacit knowledge can be possessed by itself, explicit knowledge must rely on being tacitly understood and applied, hence all knowledge is either tacit or rooted in tacit knowledge. A wholly explicit knowledge is unthinkable.*

That quote of itself questions much of the common process of knowledge management, but a true trans-disciplinary approach will add more challenges. In a short article I can simply list some insights from this trans-disciplinary work, but even a simple summary should undermine approaches to knowledge management that seek to directly measure impact. The list that follows is not intended to challenge the overall concept of measurement, but rather to say that measurement in the utilisation and deployment of knowledge, so heavily dependent on tactic elements, on experience, on intuition, and creative repurposing (exaptation in biology) cannot be measured as an asset, nor can the impact of knowledge management be isolated from other organisational practices. Direct attribution of cause and effect between a knowledge programme per se and organisational outcome is, from a scientific perspective, *a priori* impossible.

Key scientific insights

I've cherry picked some of the most immediately relevant material here, there is more and far too little attention is payed to this by people seeking simplistic recipes.

- In a meta-study of all available research on human motivation published in New Scientist we discover that 'there is no question that in virtually all circumstances in which people are doing things in order to get rewards, extrinsic tangible rewards undermine intrinsic motivation'.[1] Sharing and using knowledge is a volunteer process, highly dependent on motivation. It cannot not be forced or conscripted. To measure such activity is problematic at the best of times, but in organisations suffering from survey fatigue, and subject to increasingly short term financial pressure, it will also destroy the very thing it is trying to remember. Further knowledge is an ephemeral subject which is why too many people simply focus on information. Information use and deployment can be measured in a structured way, knowledge cannot. We can measure its impact at a localised level within context but that is a very different process. It lacks the controls of outcome based objectives that have become all too familiar in industry, and more tragically adopted in government late in their life cycle as *industrial best practice*, often after industry has realised their limitations. So rather than create an artificial and inauthentic construct we should change the granularity of what we measure and the nature of the practice we encourage. To make something fit because people expect it may have a short term advantage, but the underlying dishonesty will sooner or later come back to haunt us.

- Drew, Võ, and Wolfe report an experiment in which '24 radiologists were asked to perform a familiar lung nodule detection task. A picture of a gorilla, 48 times larger than the average nodule, was inserted in the last case. 83 per cent of radiologists did not see the gorilla. Eye-tracking showed that the majority of those who missed the gorilla looked directly at it'.[2] We do not see what we do not expect to see. In consequence we cannot trust what people say about past projects or events, nor can we assume that people will see everything in a knowledge management document, or pay attention to it even if they see it in the first place. In a series of experiments in IBM over a decade ago we ran a lessons learnt process the day before, and the day after outsourcing teams knew the results of their bid. Before the event their description of the past was contingent. After the news, if they had succeeded the story changed to one in which through insight and understanding they had done the right thing. If they had failed a series of accidents, bad luck, and poor resourcing meant that despite their best endeavours they were doomed. The documents and databases of knowledge management are at best strictly limited in their application. At worst they have little or no relevance even at the time of their creation, and less again a few years later.
- A key discovery in the US Army during the Gulf War was that platoon commanders paid more attention to the blog posts of other commanders than they did to doctrine (best practice). The real, un-mediated and un-interpreted narrative was more valuable that the distillation and summarisation of past practice or doctrine, despite the fact it took longer to read and absorb. This matches a process known as *Conceptual Blending* in human decision making. Faced with a complex set of inputs we pay attention to around five percent and match what we perceive to our own fragmented memories and those of those heard and retained in narrative form from others. It's a first fit pattern match as well, not a best fit. We then blend all of those fragments together to come up with a unique approach in context of need. Evolutionary pressure means that the early hominoids, avoiding predators on the savannah of Africa, had to make decisions very quickly based on a partial data scan, privileging their most recalled direct and vicarious experiences. Most modern knowledge management systems are based on how

computers process data, rather than on how humans have evolved to be knowledgeable.

- Percy Spencer was orphaned at the age of seven, and a grammar school drop-out at the age of 12, but his self-education propelled him into a role as one of the world's leading experts in radar tube design at Raytheon. One day while standing in front of an active radar set, the candy bar in his pocket melted. Others had noticed this heat phenomenon before, but Spencer's curiosity led him to fully investigate it. He and his colleagues decided to try heating other foods. Their investigation eventually resulted in the invention of the microwave oven. Chance discovery is the heart of knowledge creation. Structured approaches to knowledge management, especially those based on codification, are unlikely to result in such small noticings, but they are at the heart of human creativity. In biology this process of rapid re-purposing is known as exaptation. The hypo-campus evolved to manipulate muscles in fingers to allow our ancestors to pick seeds from seed pods, but in humans it has undergone a process or exaptation to manage grammar in human language. Evolution turns out to be more a matter of survival of the luckiest than it is of the fittest. IBM repurposed punch cards used to control sewing machines to create the first computer programming systems. The examples are legion – but how to you measure serendipity, chance discovery?

I have given a limited summary of a partial list of scientific facts relating to human knowledge. I could add to that a law of economics from Professor Goodhart, a former chief adviser to the Bank of England: 'As soon as the government attempts to regulate any particular set of financial assets, these become unreliable as indicators of economic trends', memorably simplified by the anthropologist Marilyn Strathern as: 'When a measure becomes a target, it ceases to be a good measure.' The danger with any measurement system is that it will be reduced to a target at which point target achievement becomes more important than the thing measured.

Even the most basic understanding of the above points would indicate to any reader that conventional approaches to measurement will not work in something as essentially human as knowledge utilisation and management. If you fall into the trap of trying to attribute direct connections between your knowledge programme and business benefit you can probably construct some impressive figures. But when resources are tight and programmes have to be cut those figures will be easily dismissed; multiple causal factors will have come into play. Knowledge and information flowed within projects and the organisation before you started to formally manage it, and it will flow again when your programme is closed. In one study within IBM we carried out ethnographic research into the use of communities of practice by experienced staff and in general they used them to find the name of someone they could have a conversation with. There are cheaper and more resilient ways of connecting people that building information databases. Old practices were manifesting and giving false data of utilisation, something that everyone knew except the knowledge management function.

New ways of thinking and acting

All however is not lost, but we need to go deeper to look at the purpose of measuring knowledge impact. Its purpose is to justify investment in the knowledge function and to protect it as an asset during times of scarcity. Many programmes are created when there is abundant resource, or a process is a fashion item in the management literature. What counts is what survives when resources are more limited, then you know what really matters. So what should we do to achieve that? Based on over two decades of experience, as a practitioner, as an academic, and as a too frequent speaker at multiple knowledge management events I think there are some basic lessons that we can learn, practices that we can adopt.

- First, shift from *lessons leant* to *lessons learning*. The retrospective and static nature of most knowledge management systems with their dependency on codification, summarisation, and hindsight makes them vulnerable to charges of irrelevance when hard decisions have to be made. Our own work in Cognitive Edge focuses on creating operational systems that capture learning in the field at the point of insight, self-interpreted at that point by the human involved, not some analytical text engine. Recall is based on 'if I knew the answer to this issue I would interpret it like this', which results in the recall of a series of fragmented direct observations that can be blended by the decision maker into a form of action. Those fragmented experiences can be linked to more formal documents and they are more likely to be read if they are discovered through narrative than a taxonomic or key word search. The more your systems are small, pragmatic, and operational the more they are a part of the *way we do things around here,* less likely to be called on to justify themselves in the first place. Such systems are rarely challenged, require little support staff, and can use existing infrastructure. Such discovery also encourages small noticings, chance discoveries key to innovation. Further it allows you to measure actual use in the field, and to measure the reflections and consequences.

- Secondly, avoid the creation of central knowledge management team and function. That marks out a cost that has to be justified and delegates the responsibility for knowledge to an isolated cost centre rather than letting it be imbedded in the business itself. A low cost admin/support function (it used be called a library and is still best staffed by librarians) supported by staff seconded part time from actual projects and activities not only makes our cost less visible but less in need of justification. It also creates a network of champions in the operational aspects of the organisation; engaged, embedded, and mixing the esoterica of formal knowledge management with the pragmatics of operational deployment. It keeps the knowledge function honest, not (as too frequently happens) isolated in its own linguistic structures and self-validating processes.
- Thirdly, avoid the use of technology in the early stages of a programme. It is expensive and requires significant expenditure and commitment. In the various knowledge projects I have run over the years we have started by matching *things that keep executives awake at night* with existing knowledge assets and capability at a micro-project/activity level rather than some grand plan. The source data for this is deployment of decision mapping journals to discover the reality of existing knowledge utilisation. Small projects then link needs with capabilities and arise from differences between the messiness of the bottom up and the formality of process maps that reflect the ideal of how things should be. This approach starts with where things are, not where people think they should be. It more effectively utilises existing capability, then acquires new methods and tools on an incremental basis linked to operational need and justified as such at the time. Over time this may create a need and justification for wider investment, but you don't start with the future. If you do that you will miss opportunities on the journey by focusing on an over structured and idealistic future state.

Now the approach I have outlined above works with the findings of science – they are organic in nature, evolutionary in trajectory. In managing knowledge we are not engineering a system but tending to a complex ecology of formal gardens and wild flower areas; the latter are preserved for genetic variety in times of stress. Efficiency has replaced effectiveness over the last two decades, and a computer model of information retrieval and distribution underpins most knowledge management systems. Such an approach lacks authenticity to our biological nature and is unsustainable under conditions of uncertainty.

Conclusion

The underlying theory behind all of this is the field of anthro-complexity, the combination of the human sciences with complex adaptive systems theory. The latter deals with systems that are inherently uncertain in nature. I've written of those in two articles, both of which are among the most cited in their field. *Complex Acts of Knowing* published in 2000[3] introduced complexity to knowledge within communities. *A Leader's Framework to Decision Making*[4] did the same for decision theory, which along with innovation should be the focus of knowledge management. The essence of complexity theory, which underpins most aspects of human systems, is that we can only manage the dispositional state of the current system, nudging it in the right direction as the opportunities present themselves. It means that we replace outcome based targets with vector measures. Vectors measure direction and speed of travel against intensity of effort. There are no linear relationships between cause and effect in a complex system, there are no recipes, no templates that provide certainty. Managing small things in the present radically reduces the vulnerability of knowledge management programmes to questions of investment, better it reflects the true nature of things.

One question I was asked at the presentation in Milan was: 'How do we create a knowledge sharing culture?' It is a question that gets asked all too frequently. My response was, as ever: 'If you have to ask the question you are starting in the wrong place.' People naturally share knowledge in the context of need. If you are having difficulty in getting people to share knowledge then your system does not reflect the natural flows of knowledge flow for which we have evolved as a species. I would advocate the same in the context of this article; if you have to cost justify a knowledge function then you have not built it in the right way. It's not too late to take a naturalistic approach; small activities, linked to real world problems, justified as part of those activities – not in abstract.

References

1. Flemming, N., "The bonus myth: How paying for results can backfire", New Scientist, Issue 2807, 9th April 2011, pp. 40–43
2. Drew, T., Võ, M., and Wolfe, J., "The Invisible Gorilla Strikes Again: Sustained Inattentional Blindness in Expert Observers", Psychological Science, Volume 24 No. 9, Sep. 2013, pp. 1848–1853
3. Snowden, D., "Complex Acts of Knowing", Journal of Knowledge Management, Vol. 6, No. 2, May 2000, pp. 100–111
4. Snowden, D., and Boone, M., "A Leaders Framework to Decision Making", Havard Business Review, Nov. 2007

www.ingramcontent.com/pod-product-compliance
Ingram Content Group UK Ltd.
Pitfield, Milton Keynes, MK11 3LW, UK
UKHW021848150926
8657IPUK00005B/145

9 781783 582686